MW00772887

ALLIGATOR TEARS

ALLIGATOR TEARS

A Memoir in Essays

EDGAR GOMEZ

CROWN
NEW YORK

Published in the United States by Crown, an imprint of the Crown Publishing Group, a division of Penguin Random House LLC, New York.
crownpublishing.com

CROWN and the Crown colophon are registered trademarks of Penguin Random House LLC.

Chapter 7, "My Boyfriend, His Lover, and Me," was originally published in slightly different form under the same title in *The Rumpus,* December 2020.

Library of Congress Cataloging-in-Publication Data
Names: Gomez, Edgar (Writer), author.
Title: Alligator tears: a memoir in essays / Edgar Gomez.
Description: First edition. | New York: Crown, [2025]
Identifiers: LCCN 2024015912 | ISBN 9780593728543 (hardcover) |
ISBN 9780593728550 (ebook)
Classification: LCC HQ75.8.G72 A3 2025 |
DDC 306.76/62092 [B]—dc23/eng/20240529
LC record available at https://lccn.loc.gov/2024015912

Hardcover ISBN 978-0-593-72854-3
Ebook ISBN 978-0-593-72855-0

Printed in the United States of America on acid-free paper

Editor: Aubrey Martinson
Production editor: Liana Faughnan
Text designer: Amani Shakrah
Production manager: Dustin Amick
Copy editor: Janet Biehl
Proofreaders: Andrea C. Peabbles, Eldes Tran,
Sibylle Kazeroid, Miriam Taveras
Publicist: Bree Martinez
Marketer: Rachel Rodriguez

1 3 5 7 9 8 6 4 2

First Edition

For Rudy,
who was always there.
Miss you, cuz.

What cannot be said will be wept.

—Sappho

I wanna be wealthy. If not wealthy:
content, comfortable. I wanna be somebody.
I mean, I *am* somebody. I just wanna be
a rich somebody.

—Octavia St. Laurent, *Paris Is Burning*

CONTENTS

ALLIGATOR TEARS

1

ORLANDO ROYALTY

It happened on a weekday, around eight-thirty p.m. I remember because *America's Next Top Model* was on. My older brother, Hector, stormed into the living room and yanked me up by the arm without saying a word. Seconds later we were in Mom's room, standing at the foot of her bed, where she lay shivering and twisting her head from side to side, strands of her copper-tinted hair glued to her sweaty forehead, dark roots growing like weeds along the edges. "¿Dónde están? I want to go. I don't understand," she kept saying. Her eyelids fluttered open and closed, as if she were coming in and out of a bad dream. "I can't feel anything. Where are they? I'm cold."

My stepdad, Omar, was seated next to her. "Go to your mother," he told me.

Seeing the panic in Omar's eyes, how small and scared he looked in his boxers and an old, baggy tank top, I had to stop myself from laughing at him. Since marrying Mom, the only times he'd acknowledged I existed were when he was telling her how soft I was, that she'd better put me in sports with other boys before she ended up raising a little girl. Now look who was acting like a "little girl." And for what? It's not like Mom was dying. People didn't die out of nowhere. She was just . . . having a nightmare. Or okay, maybe she was sick, but give her some ginger tea and VapoRú and she'd be back to normal in no time. Come on, didn't he know her at all?

Annoyed with Hector for dragging me away from the TV for whatever this was, I tried to revive the excitement I'd felt moments earlier watching *Top Model*. My favorite contestant, Eva, had performed well in the week's challenge. Despite her fear of spiders, she'd remained not only calm but beautiful while modeling diamonds with a live tarantula crawling on her face. I wanted to see her reaction when she won. I imagined Tyra revealing her photo as the week's top contestant, a scene I could've been watching back in the living room, when suddenly Mom began to groan. It was in response to Hector, who'd climbed into the bed to shake her by the shoulders, his round, pudgy cheeks streaked with tears. The sight of him threw me.

My brother never cried.

He was fifteen. I was twelve.

"Levantese," Hector pleaded at Mom. "Wake up! Don't go to sleep!"

With each word that spilled out of my brother's mouth, the reality that something might actually be wrong became harder to avoid. Writhing on top of her sweat-soaked bedsheets, Mom muttered more gibberish. "It's . . . okay," she insisted. "I can't feel my legs." She turned abruptly to Omar. "Who are *you*?"

The color drained out of his dark brown face. He bowed his head in prayer.

"Diosito, por favor no dejes que esta . . ."

I took a step back toward the door. I had to get back to Eva. I needed to be there when she won. Whatever was going on here wasn't real. Mom couldn't be dying . . . because no . . . because then, who would cut our hair? Or yell at us to close the windows when the AC was on? Who would burst into my room at 2:02 in the morning of my birthday every year, jump onto my bed, and shout, "Guess what your mamá was doing at this exact minute?"

"Should we call an ambulance?" Hector cried out.

No one answered him. Not me, or Omar, or my cousin Dante. He'd been so quiet, I hadn't noticed he was in the room with us, held hostage by a portrait of Jesus nailed to the wall. Dante shifted his eyes from Hector's terrified face to Omar's to mine, waiting for one of us to move.

It horrifies me to admit it now, but right then, what I was standing there thinking was:

How much does an ambulance cost?

"No." Omar's voice cut through the silence. "She said she's okay."

I didn't know whether to believe him. Mom *did* say she was okay, but that couldn't possibly be true, could it? I suspect we were both hoping the same thing: that all of a sudden she would sit up, yawn, and stretch her arms wide, then look at us crowded around her and say, "What's going on? Why is everyone in here? An ambulance? ¡Están locos! You know how expensive those are? I was just sleeping! ¡No lo puedo creer! Who was going to pay for that? I can't even close my eyes for five seconds without this house falling apart!"

Caught between worrying she'd get mad at me if I called for help that she didn't need and seeing her struggle to stay awake as Hector wept over her body, I held on to the edge of her bed, my knees crumbling under the weight of me.

Please, I begged the universe, God, anyone who might be listening. *It's just a fever, right? It's just pneumonia?* I'd had it a few years before and had similarly lain awake all night shivering and stringing senseless words together. I vaguely remembered Mom hovering over me, pressing a cool cloth to my burning forehead. No one said anything about taking me to a hospital then. Somewhere deep down in my subconscious, I had understood she needed me to fight it on my own. "I'm okay," I'd said too. I wasn't, but a few days later I was fine.

Mom would be fine. She had to be.

Hours passed, though it couldn't have been more than a minute.

Then, in a flash, Dante barged out of the room, returning moments later with the announcement that he'd called an ambulance. Instantly, Hector, Omar, and I jumped into action: packing an overnight bag, clearing the way for a gurney, assuring Mom that everything was going to be all right. One second there was only us, the next there were sirens, a fire truck, dirty boots scuffing up the tile floor. Men carried Mom into an ambulance. Omar climbed in after her. Hector, Dante, and I stood alone in the yard, watching the blue-red lights trail off down the block. And that was it. She was gone, and it was dark again.

Dante pressed his palm onto my shoulder. "Let's go, primo."

The three of us walked back into the house, where *Top Model* was still stupidly playing on the TV. I shut it off, went to my room, and waited in bed all night for her to come home.

Just a few years earlier, we were living in Miami.

It was a simpler time then. In the early 2000s, N*Sync and Destiny's Child had new songs out on the radio. All the movies were about aliens, robots, and skinny white ladies fighting for their equal rights. The Taco Bell mascot was a chihuahua with a Mexican accent.

My mother waited tables at a café in the Miami airport, and my father worked as a line cook at a hotel restaurant. In their wedding pictures, Mom is wearing a cream-colored dress with pointy shoulder pads, Papi's hair is picked out into a short 'fro. They look tan and scared and happy. Papi had immigrated to the United States from Puerto Rico in the 1980s as part of the latest wave of natives pushed out of the island due to rising costs of living, and Mom had come from Nicaragua fleeing the political unrest spreading through Central America. After Hector and I were born, Mom begged my grandma to come from Nica to help take care of us. Abuela probably wasn't the best babysitter, but she was fun. Every morning she slathered me with cocoa butter from head to toe, served us each a big, steaming cup of café con leche, then lifted me up and placed me inside the little metal shopping cart she pulled behind her everywhere, and we'd walk through the noisy Miami streets picking up aluminum cans to sell at the city's recycling center by the pound. Sometimes, to make extra money, we filled a couple of the cans with rocks to make them weigh more, the two of us giggling like it was a game.

Us against the world.

Simple.

At least for a little while. I mean, this was Florida after all, and though I'd loved our life there so far, some bullshit was bound to happen. Practically overnight, Papi got fired from the restaurant, then the whispers began about him being addicted to crack, maxing out the credit cards.

I was in elementary school at the time, too young to fully follow what was going on. The divorce was like a telenovela: everybody kept crying and talking really fast in Spanish, and whenever I tried to find out what was happening, I got shushed and told to go play outside. So that's what I did. I wasn't even sure what a divorcio or *crack* was. I guess I figured if any of it was important, someone would come let me know. Then one morning I woke up and Abuela was gone, back to Nica. Not long after that, Papi returned to Puerto Rico. We were in Mom's pickup truck with all our stuff in suitcases, pulling out of the driveway for the last time, when she started talking to Hector and me about how we should behave at our uncle's house.

"You have to listen to your tío," she said. "You have to be good boys, okay?"

At some point, she must have told us she'd be dropping us

off with him for a while, but it hadn't registered to me what she meant until then. I felt embarrassed, like I hadn't been paying enough attention, and now everyone was leaving me. No more walks with Abuela, no more trips to the gas station for cigarettes and lotto scratch-offs with Papi, even Mom was going somewhere. The backs of my eyes grew hot. I lowered my head as tears blurred my vision. I didn't want her to think I was a baby.

I was eight.

"You going to miss your mamá?" she looked down at me.

I turned to Hector to follow his lead. My brother stared straight ahead, the hard expression on his face revealing nothing, but he was closer to Papi than I was to Abuela.

"No," I answered her.

It was quiet in the car, then Mom leaped over the divider and wrapped her arms around me. "That's not nice," she said. "You don't have to miss me"—she kissed my head and cheek and nose, her nails digging into my sides as she squeezed me close—"but I'm going to miss you, niño. *I'm* going to miss *you.*"

· I thought we'd maybe have to stay at Tío's for a few weeks, but it ended up being almost an entire year before Mom finally picked us up again and drove us four hours north to Orlando. Apparently she'd been living there in a motel with Omar— some man she married in secret while we were apart—and now we would be too. I didn't understand who this Omar guy was or how moving into a dumb motel with a stranger was better than being with our father, even if he was on drugs, but I was too relieved to be together again to do anything but just go with it. Omar wouldn't last anyway, I told myself. Papi would come for us.

As the months passed and I waited for him to call and tell us his plan, the motel slowly began to grow on me: there were lots of tourists' kids to run around with; we all slept in one room, like camping, but with free HBO. Plus the lobby had these giant couches where you could sit as long as you wanted reading the glossy brochures for Disney World and Gatorland and the Titanic Experience that they kept out for guests, like my own personal library. Mom had found a job at the airport Starbucks and distracted us from our empty mini-fridge and the creepy people partying in the parking lot with icy Frappuccinos and thick, sticky slices of lemon cake that she smuggled out of work tucked inside the folds of her green apron.

After the motel, we bounced back and forth between Miami and Orlando trying to find affordable housing. By the time I was in the sixth grade, I'd transferred from Kinloch Park Elementary to Durrance to Sweetwater to Durrance again to Conway Middle School, clinging to the books a teacher had given me as a gift when she saw that I liked to read. The best ones were a set of fictional diaries written by real princesses from throughout history: Anastasia of Russia, whose mom sewed diamonds and jewels into her dresses to make them bulletproof, Marie Antoinette of France, who had a cute dog.

Books gave me a sense of stability that was missing from my life—as long as I had one with me, it didn't matter where I was, I could open it up, and there'd always be the same story waiting for me inside, the same people and places, which was more than I could say about the real world, where one year we slept on relatives' spare beds and the next on mattresses on the floor in ugly, beige roach-infested apartments.

Eventually Mom scraped together enough money for a down payment and went to the bank to apply for one of the predatory, high-interest loans they were giving everybody at the time. With that, she bought a small fixer-upper a five-minute drive from the Orlando airport for us to settle down in. Our first month in the house, she sprayed bleach on the black mold growing out of leaks in the ceiling, planted avocado and aloe in the yard, painted the outside walls sky blue, the driveway the brightest shade of red. All our neighbors hung flags on their windows: Dominican, Haitian, Puerto Rican. But our whole house was like a piece of Nicaragua in Florida.

Still, Mom could barely manage the mortgage payments. She'd spend night after night arguing in her bedroom with Omar about the rent he was supposed to help with, the rotten pipes he'd sworn to fix, where he'd been when he stumbled home past midnight reeking of liquor again.

"Out with one of your putas?" she sobbed. "This isn't a motel! You can't just come and go whenever you want! You promised you were different! You told me you loved—"

"You're fucking crazy!" Omar's voice boomed through the house's thin walls. "Trying to *trap* me! Watch what you say, Teresa, if it weren't for me, who would you have, huh, WHO?"

There were other nights, though, when I'd walk into the living room and find them snuggled up on the couch, watching telenovelas or whatever crappily dubbed Arnold Schwarzenegger movie Telemundo was airing. They could be there for hours, Omar cussing at the screen, Mom's head resting on his shoulder, a cozy smile on her face. Seeing them that way scared me more than when they fought, because it's when I first realized they really did love each other. It's when I realized this was it, our new life, and Papi was never coming back.

I should tell you about my cousin Dante now.

He was Tío Ramon's teenage son, the uncle Hector and I had lived with in Miami for a year. From the outside, our family must have appeared to be doing better—with the house and everything—because one night Mom told us my cousin had called her asking if he could come stay with us for a bit. His timing was terrible, we were only just getting on our feet in Orlando, but Mom said yes, I suppose to return the favor to Tío for letting us stay with him in the past.

Dante was Miami through and through. He swooped in wearing a puka shell necklace and flip-flops, his long, dark hair in frizzy cornrows, talking about "When are we going out? Where do y'all wanna go?" as if he thought living in Orlando would be a vacation. I was so excited to have another big brother around that I ran to show him the bedroom we'd be sharing and the bunk bed Mom had gotten for us at the flea market so we wouldn't have to sleep on mattresses on the floor anymore. Dante sat on the bottom bunk, blinked looking around at the cramped room and the wrinkled brochures I'd pinned to the wall as art, and let out a deflated, "Oh."

For a while after he arrived, Mom tried to maintain the illusion that we were doing okay. Weekends she took us to do the free things in town: to the beach and M&M's store at the mall, to see the nighttime fireworks display at Downtown Disney. We went on tours of timeshares because they gave you all-you-could-eat continental breakfast and tickets to theme parks if you sat through a three-hour-long sales pitch. ("I'm sorry, I can't make decisions like this without my husband present!" she told the real estate agents the second they handed over our tickets. Then we all stomped away holding back laughs.) That was how I got to ride a roller coaster for the first time. Until then we'd only driven by them on the highway, my face glued to the window, watching in awe as the long rows of track curved and loop-de-looped across the sky like the spines of giant magical beasts. But soon we reverted to our regular routines, hardly ever doing any of that touristy stuff.

Mom woke up at three a.m. every morning to go open the airport Starbucks and worked till late in the afternoon, came home, cooked and cleaned, then fell into bed bone-tired and in a deep fog from the endless pills she took for her various pains and headaches.

Omar mostly stayed in the yard, fixing up junk cars and re-selling them while he was between jobs, or else he was out all night, no one knew where.

Early on when Dante moved in, they tried not to argue around him, but it didn't take long before their fights resumed in full force. The plate smashing, the slurred threats. Mom whimpering alone in her bedroom for hours after Omar stormed out of the house. "I'm fine. I'm fine. Go to sleep," she'd tell us when we knocked on her door to check on her.

Afterward a hush fell over the house, as if we were all afraid the slightest sound might trigger another explosion. Dante would bring the kitchen phone to our room and settle into the bottom bunk, and I'd climb to the bunk above him. Moments later I'd hear him nervously whispering to his parents, his private, unfiltered thoughts rising up to me like smoke: how much Orlando sucked compared to Miami, that we lived in the ghetto, and the AC was constantly broken, and Mom and Omar were going to kill each other and nobody cared, and—

"Can you send me twenty dollars for pizza?" he'd ask. "I'm hungry. They eat like, once a day. What she cooks, and the rest is Starbucks . . . my stomach hurts."

Why don't you go back to your own house then! I always wanted to stick my head out and yell. *Since you hate it here so much!* Instead I lay there pretending to sleep, too embarrassed to admit that what he was saying sounded kind of true.

Before Dante moved in with us, I was aware our family was struggling, but I didn't have a lot to compare my life to. My only frames of reference were the bits and pieces our uncles and aunts had shared with my brother and me about their childhoods in Nicaragua during the dictatorship and civil war, walking miles on foot through dirt roads to get to school, dead bodies lining the gutters, the hunger and violence and kids ripped from their parents' arms. Whenever I got frustrated with something, I reminded myself that things could always be worse. At least we weren't in a motel anymore. At least Mom, Hector, and me were together again.

I didn't see the point in bothering anyone with my trivial first-world feelings, especially when Mom was clearly doing her best to keep us afloat. Because Hector never complained and the adults closest to me acted like nothing was ever wrong, I accepted our lives as they were. But listening to my cousin's calls to his parents, for once I heard an echo of my own stifled frustrations, and all the memories from over the years that I'd tried convincing myself were "adventures" or "not that bad" replayed in my mind in their original, unembellished bleakness. Collecting dirty cans inside Abuela's rickety cart. Hiding in the lobby while Mom and Omar fought in our motel room. The fact that my teacher had only given me books because she caught me stealing from the library.

It was around this time that I began to harbor a secret fantasy that I'd been adopted, and soon my real parents, royals in a country far away, would pick me up and apologize for dumping me on some poor family. *Why did you abandon me?* I'd ask, and they'd smile tenderly and say they didn't want to; it was necessary so that I'd learn humility and grow up to be a good ruler.

In retrospect, those nights I spent lying in the bed above Dante, wondering why he didn't go back to Miami already, I was just jealous. It was easy for him to point out all our problems. For him, this *was* a vacation, but I was stuck here.

One afternoon, just a few months before my cousin would call the ambulance for us, I came home from school and found the front door thrown open, swaying softly in the breeze.

Inside, a handful of leaves had blown in from the yard and lay scattered across the first few feet of tile floor, baking like tourists under the beams of sunlight that made it through the door. But beyond them, the place was dark, quieter than normal. Mom wasn't in the kitchen, where she usually was after work. I looked around, confused. At this time of day, the house should have been full of the voices of people on the telenovelas always playing on TV, screaming and threatening each other in Spanish. That's when it hit me it wasn't just their voices missing—the TV itself was gone. Clumps of dirt curled around the spot on the living room floor where it used to sit, trailing off past the welcome mat outside.

"Mamá?" I whispered.

She didn't answer.

I backed up to the front door. Behind me, cars clambered up and down the street. I stood there, trying to decide whether to stay inside or go flag someone down. Then I shook the thought away and grabbed the strap of my backpack, holding on tight as I moved slowly down the hallway to her bedroom. *Stop being a little bitch,* I scolded myself. *She's probably just sleeping.*

"Mamá?" I repeated louder.

Still no answer.

When I reached her door, I wrapped my fingers around the doorknob. Before I could chicken out, I pushed it open.

My eyes darted around the room in a panic. It looked like a hurricane had ripped through it. Her mattress was flipped over, thrown sloppily against the wall, the painting of Jesus that'd been hanging there knocked down. Her dresser drawers were yanked out of their slots and hung slack-jawed from their hinges. Every inch of the floor was covered with pieces of torn mail, bras and socks and panties. Right as I was about to shut the door and run outside to get help, I heard a faint, scratching noise nearby, like a rake being dragged over concrete.

"Mamá?" I tried one last time.

Finally she yelled back, "I'm in here!"

I rushed toward her voice coming from the tiny half-bathroom connected to her bedroom, imagining a thousand kidnapping scenarios I'd have to rescue her from. In the bathroom, however, I found Mom unharmed, her Starbucks uniform still on. She was hunched over a broom, sweeping up bits of glass into a dustpan, the window above her head shattered except for a few shards clinging to the edges of the frame, threatening to break off any second.

"What happened?" I asked, scanning her appearance for signs of struggle. But there were no tears running down her cheeks. Her rust-colored hair was wrestled back into a ponytail, not a strand out of place. Yet there was something unmistakably off about her, staring at the pile of glass by her feet with a worn-down look in her eyes as if she wanted to lie down beside it.

Mom pointed her bottom lip at the broken window. Past the shards of glass, the leafy branches of the orange tree in our yard stretched out toward the sky.

"That's how they got in," Mom said.

"Who?" I asked.

"I don't know." She sighed and lowered her head again to resume sweeping. "Someone who's been watching us. Someone who knew we wouldn't be home."

I moved closer to the window, trying to picture how anybody could climb in through there. It didn't make sense. What did she mean, someone was watching us? What was so special about our house? Then I remembered the front door—had she left it open in case she needed to run too? I waited for her to say more, but she simply kept on sweeping as if I wasn't there. The orange tree's fractured shadow rippled along the wall behind her. It was obvious she wanted to be alone.

When later that night I asked if she'd called the police, Mom shrugged and said she did, but that it wouldn't matter. She was cooking dinner and didn't move her eyes from the thinly sliced plantains sizzling in a pan of hot oil on the stove, her mascara melting inside the rising smoke fumes. "Those people," Mom scoffed, prodding the plantains with a fork. "They don't care."

She'd barely said a word since I'd found her. All afternoon she'd been like a ghost, roaming from room to room slamming doors, throwing drawers open, cataloging what we lost with loud, painful-sounding groans. The burglar took the TV, the bootleg cable box, our passports, the radio, all the cash Mom kept under her mattress, and most of her jewelry, leaving her with just the cross around her neck and the Chinese beaded bracelet she always wore for good luck.

"But what if they come back?" I asked cautiously.

"Don't make me think about that." She waved me away.

"Are you going to cover the window?"

"Later." She dropped the plantains onto a plate, covered them with a napkin, then lifted the frying pan and began pouring the hot vegetable oil into a coffee mug to reuse the next day.

"Did the police say who they think it was?"

"Not yet."

"Did they say what they're going to do?"

"Please. Not now. I'm busy."

I hated when she got like this, treating me like a child, never telling me what was going on. She couldn't expect me to stay quiet forever, like the robbery wasn't any of my business.

"Well, what *did* they tell you?" I pressed on.

"¡Ay!" She yelped as a drop of hot oil popped out of the pan and seared her skin, joining dozens of other burns along her tan arms. "See what happens when you bother me when I'm cooking! ¡Ya, por favor, déjame terminar! I can't focus! Diosito, ayúdame, what did I do to deserve this? ¡Ya me tienen hasta el colmo en esta maldita casa! One of these days I'm going to die and you're going to say, 'Boo hoo! I miss my poor mom! I wish I helped her. I wish I gave her a break . . . ' Pero no. I work all day and come home to try and rest and I can't even have that!"

"Okaaay," I muttered under my breath, walking away before she could launch into her favorite rant about how sorry I'd be at her funeral that I didn't take out the trash more.

A week later the police ended their investigation. "Probably someone from the neighborhood," they said. "Second break-in this month. High-crime area." They asked Mom if she even wanted to file a report, considering how little the stolen property added up to. She was right. They didn't care.

That Sunday, she boarded up the window with a slab of plywood from Home Depot, dug up an ADT home security sign from somewhere and planted it on the lawn to trick people into believing we paid for the service. The next, an uncle drove up from Miami to change the locks and gave us his old, clunky TV set we put where the old one was in the living room.

Without the box we'd been using to steal cable from our neighbors, we were stuck watching the boring free public channels. I was flipping through them one night when my eyes landed on a reality competition show I'd never heard of before. It was brighter than all the others, hypnotizing. The drama. The brutal fashion industry experts. The absurd photoshoots Tyra forced the contestants to do for a coveted CoverGirl contract. I was hooked instantly. Absorbed in the glow of *America's Next Top Model,* my surroundings faded away, and I forgot that somebody had torn up our house just as we were beginning to get comfortable in it, about the nightmares I'd been having that the burglar would slip in through my window next, how in the latest, he tied me to my bed and slid a knife up and down my belly, laughing before bending over and kissing me on the lips. I watched the girls try to stay calm while posing with tarantulas and for an hour, nothing could touch me. I was safe.

After a few days at the hospital, we brought Mom home in a wheelchair, bundled up in blankets and unable to stand for long periods on her own. Half of her face was paralyzed. Her left cheek and lips drooped half an inch, like melted wax over a flame, a condition known as Bell's palsy. Her eye suffered the most damage. It drooped too, and because of the paralysis, she had trouble blinking, which made her tear up at random even when she wasn't sad about anything. At least that's what she'd say for the next couple of years every time I found her crying.

The final diagnosis was a stroke. Stress-induced. Mom had always told us she was exhausted, that between her job and our laziness, we were killing her. But I thought all moms talked like that. I assumed, because she'd been carrying our family on her shoulders all my life, that she could take it. Besides, for years I'd overheard my aunts reassuring her that rainy days were temporary and things were bound to improve. *God is looking out for you,* they said, and *You can't depend on men. You have to be their mom and dad. Stay strong, Tere.*

Maybe she could have, but the burglary had been her limit. Decades later Mom would confide in me that she'd been planning a special Christmas for us, had been saving her cash tips from Starbucks all year. She'd felt bad about the divorce and the motel and making us use the Mane 'n Tail horse shampoo she bought in bulk instead of like, regular Pantene or whatever. She wanted to do something nice for us. When she discovered the burglar took all of the money she'd strained to set aside one dollar at a time, she was devastated. Not only was there nothing left for Christmas, now we were *those people* who lived in the house with wood nailed over the window. Mom began to work doubles, weekends, desperate to save enough to start over again, but there's only so much a body already running at capacity can do. Raising her two kids, and Dante, on her own on nine dollars an hour. Panicking nonstop over house payments. Sleeping three, four hours a night.

She broke, trying to keep us together, because everyone pushed her to be strong.

The doctor said we'd have to be gentle with her and make sure she got plenty of rest. Guilty for being useless during the stroke, I became her diligent nurse throughout her recovery. I microwaved her tea to take her medicine with, tucked her in when the pills made her drowsy, plucked the white hairs from her scalp, escorted her to the bathroom, made us tuna sandwiches and ramen. We passed weeks burritoed together on the couch in her favorite fuzzy tiger-print blanket watching *Caso Cerrado* and *Family Feud* marathons. My mother, who loved bloody steak and chased the snakes out of our backyard with a machete, trembled holding up the remote.

At school, my teachers made little comments about my falling weight and lack of focus, but who cares about history when you've seen your mom in a hospital bed with a million tubes and things sticking out of her? How could I draw a stupid family tree when one of my parents was on CRACK, the other could barely move her FACE, and my so-called stepdad was drunk all day, pissed off we'd invaded his territory like a weird brown SHREK? I didn't tell any of my teachers she was sick, worried they'd call home or make me go to talk to a counselor. What were they going to say anyway? *Stay strong.* Be serious.

Dante stayed in Orlando for a short while to help out around the house, then returned to Miami when Mom's condition improved a bit. For months, I'd resented my cousin for all the nights he'd made me listen to him tell his parents everything that was wrong with us, and yet once he was gone, all I felt toward him was gratitude, because he saved her. While Hector, Omar, and I had all stood frozen at the foot of Mom's bed, calculating the cost and risk of calling an ambulance, he did what none of us would. If Dante hadn't been there, if we hadn't been lucky, we might have wasted even more precious time before calling one. He was the only one willing to be honest that there was something wrong, that we needed help. Before him, I'd blindly followed the adults around me, moving through my life in a naïve daze, hoping they knew where we were going.

Now I understood that hope wasn't enough. I couldn't rely on hoping that if Mom had another stroke, someone would magically appear to rescue her. No, I had to. I had to get rich and make it up to her that I'd hesitated by guaranteeing that being poor would never be a problem again.

After Dante left, Hector and I tried making money however we could, selling chocolate bars to our neighbors, gathering all the junk from around the house and throwing a yard sale. Both attempts were failures: in our neighborhood, people didn't open their doors to strangers, much less shop on each other's lawns. In the end, we asked Mom to let us borrow her truck to go set up a booth at the flea market. Every Saturday and Sunday, my brother and I woke up at the crack of dawn and drove to the empty field an hour away where it was held. Hector handled the sales, while I stood by trying to look sad and needy, luring in customers like in a depressing charity commercial. It worked. We made enough to stock the fridge, fill the gas tank. It was at the flea market that I learned people are more likely to help you if they feel sorry for you.

Because my bed was lower to the ground than hers and not as difficult to get into, Mom started sleeping in my room with me. She could sleep whole days away in there, like she was catching up for all the years she'd lost. At night, I'd tiptoe up to the bed, slide under the sheets, and rest my arm lightly around her belly, pressing my nose to her back to inhale the scent of cocoa butter and sweat on her skin. "La quiero mucho," I'd say into the darkness, and every now and then she'd surprise me by turning around and groggily saying it back. In the morning, we'd wake up facing away from each other—it was too hot to sleep hugging—but there'd always be a small piece of me touching her: my foot grazing the back of her thigh, a finger poking into her arm. Something to send a signal to my brain that her body was still next to mine. Mamá, my queen. I can't believe there was ever a time I thought she'd abandoned me.

At some point during her recovery, Mom's insurance approved Botox injections as a treatment for her Bell's palsy. By then she was able to walk and drive on her own again, though she rarely left the house other than for groceries or urgent errands, and only hidden behind a pair of giant black sunglasses to conceal her drooping cheek and eye.

The day of her first treatment, I sat beside her on the exam table, squeezing her hand while the doctor drew X's on her face to mark where the Botox would go. The two of us were buzzing with nerves. It was all vaguely glamorous; the waiting room had been full of rich ladies with designer handbags and huge pouty lips. When the doctor was done marking Mom up, he went to a table to prepare the needles. I didn't know how long they'd be until then. Thick. I squeezed her hand tighter as he began to flick each needle with the tip of his index finger and push the air out, drops of Botox falling to the floor like venom. My heart raced; there had to have been a dozen X's on her face. If she was frightened too, she didn't show it.

"Are you scared?" Mom asked, looking down at me.

I shook my head fast, no.

She stared at me a long second, then leaned over and whispered in a funny accent, "Don't you know your mom is a model? I have to get ready for my photoshoot in *Paris, darling*."

I lowered my eyes. I wasn't sure what to say, if it was okay to joke like that at the doctor's. I was about to turn thirteen—too old to be playing games.

"What about you, niño?" Mom asked. She poked my shoulder. "You're not a model?"

I kept my eyes on the floor, but still, for the fun of it, I imagined myself on TV. Tyra holding out my photo and announcing me as the week's winner. It would have been cool.

"I guess," I shrugged, blushing.

"Well duh." She pointed at her face. At the Bell's palsy. "You got your looks from me!"

I tried not to laugh as Mom kissed my cheek and shook my arm, forcing an embarrassed smile out of me. "You don't have to be scared," she said. I leaned my head against her shoulder, closing my eyes when the doctor approached with the first needle. Tyra reached out a hand, pulling me toward her. The rest of the appointment passed by in an easy, breezy, beautiful blur.

2

KIDS WITH GUNS

My mom didn't trust other people's kids enough to let me go out anywhere, but I didn't really have friends anyway. In 2005 I turned thirteen and started high school. A week before classes began, I sat in the bathroom holding back tears while Mom chopped my long, messy black curls down to an inch, one of the requirements of the new criminal justice program I'd enrolled in. That year, I was bald, desperate, and stuck at home most days looking for something to do.

My latest source of distraction was the old Microsoft computer we kept shoved into a corner of the kitchen, where for years it had stayed shut off, gathering dust. It might have been nice once, but by the time we inherited it from some tío, it had missing letters on the keyboard, fossilized bugs trapped behind the screen. Even when we were robbed, the burglar didn't bother taking it. I would've ignored it too if we hadn't recently gotten the Internet.

Soon enough I discovered anything worth doing in person was available online, except better: for free. You could window-shop for clothes on designer websites without being followed around a store by pushy salespeople. You could sneak into adult chat rooms and seduce married men, then tell them your age and that they were going to HELL. You could be anyone.

On Myspace, I told strangers all over the world my name was Luis Lush. Technically I was catfishing, but just barely. Luis wasn't that far off from the real me. I used actual photos of myself, only from before my ugly haircut. Decorated my profile with GIFs of twinkling diamonds. Listed my interests as Madonna (who I didn't dare listen to in public), New York (where I'd never been), and coffee (which I drank by the potful, staying up past three a.m. sending hot guys friend requests). My sexual orientation I left blank, the code that I saw all the other boys like me were using, how we let each other know what we were without fearing our family might stumble across our profiles and see the three-letter word that might ruin everything.

The person I was in the criminal justice program was the real catfish. Since enrolling, the program pretty much ruled my entire life. On Wednesdays we had to wear military fatigues to campus. Fridays: button-up shirts, loafers, and ties. No hair past the tops of our ears. No piercings. No jewelry. But as Luis Lush, I could be myself. Or at least who I wanted to be.

One morning I woke up to a new message in my Myspace inbox.

Hi lol, the subject read. In the body were two short lines: *Your cute. Wassup?* The profile picture showed a tan boy with spiky jet-black hair. He looked like a young Romeo Santos. I chewed my nails, hiding a smile as if he could see me.

Lol thanks sexy, you too, I finally typed back. *Chilling. You?*

A minute later he still hadn't replied. While I waited to see if he'd log on, I skimmed through his profile.

Josh, the display name said. I read through the few lines of his About Me that mentioned he liked "music and having fun," and then I got to his location: Orlando.

Oh, I cringed. Suddenly the excitement I'd felt a second earlier vanished. I'd talked to other boys online before, but always in another state, never with anybody physically close to my house or my mom or anything that mattered to me. Too risky. I went to hit block, but changed my mind, deciding that wouldn't be necessary and I'd simply ignore him if he ever responded.

Yet throughout the rest of the day, as I sat through my criminal justice classes listening to our teacher lecture us on the differences between prison and jail, misdemeanors and felonies, my thoughts drifted away, imagining times when we might have been at the same place, the two of us in the cereal aisle at the grocery store moments apart, missing each other by a few seconds. Just to see what it'd look like, I scribbled his name in the corner of the paper I'd been taking notes on. *Josh.*

No one in class noticed—they kept their eyes on the board. It felt good, having something secret and valuable, something more than they thought the quiet, brown kid could have. By the end of class, I'd erased Josh's name, but a part of me already knew. If he messaged me again, I was going to write back.

When I first heard about the program, I was in the eighth grade, the future far enough away that anything was possible. There were occasionally nights when I dreamt of yachts and mansions, but most of my dreams were way more ordinary than that: in one recurring fantasy of adulthood, I worked a regular nine-to-five at a cubicle in an office inputting numbers into spreadsheets. I never considered being *happy* at my job. All I cared about was making the minimum to afford a car and an apartment where no one would bother me. The problem was, I didn't understand how to get there.

That is, I didn't understand until a recruiter visited my middle school to talk about what a great opportunity studying criminal justice would be, especially for those of us preparing to go to Oak Ridge, the underfunded high school my neighborhood was zoned for, which was basically one visit from the health inspector away from being converted into a check cashing/payday loan place. If we applied to the program, though, the recruiter said we'd get to attend one of the best schools in the city: Boone. They had a *pool,* he told us. Our senior year, they'd take us on a free trip to *Washington*! Think of how amazing that would look on our *résumés*!

It seemed like a good plan to me. Boone would lead to college, then with my degree, I'd secure my sweet cubicle job and have all the money I could ever possibly need. Easy. I even thought learning about criminal justice could be fun. I figured we'd twirl toy rifles and march around wearing cute little berets, like in one of my favorite Disney movies, *Cadet Kelly*.

But the program was nothing like *Cadet Kelly*.

The program was, in fact, very serious.

Our head instructor, Ms. Roth, was a retired police officer who walked with a limp because she'd been shot in the leg during a home drug raid—a story she repeated often, I suppose to inspire us to join her in the fight to rid the streets of dangerous marijuana. Worse, I assumed other kids from my block would apply to go to Boone for a so-called better education, but because the program didn't provide buses for students from my side of town, we had to find our own transportation. I was the only one who did, thanks to Hector, who agreed to drive me.

My first day in the program, I was horrified to discover all the other criminal justice students were white kids who were zoned for Boone anyway and genuinely wanted to be cops. After one found out where I lived and asked if I was in a gang, I said, "A *gang*?!" and laughed, thinking he was kidding. When I realized he wasn't, I stopped speaking to any of my classmates. I didn't like them, and I knew they didn't like me, because they looked down when I walked by their desks to my own in the back of our classroom, like they were waiting for a ghost to pass.

Even so, I made sure to work hard. To earn straight A's. To not make a fuss or complain. At that age, I believed that's what I needed to do to get ahead. Dropping out would have gotten me labeled a quitter on my permanent record, but staying proved I was willing to pull myself up by my literal combat bootstraps. It was easier to believe that I had some control over what was happening to me, that I had a say in writing the story of my life, than confront the reality that I was following in the footsteps of millions of poor kids who are indoctrinated into the armed forces with promises of education and stability, that my story had been written long before me.

After school, I wanted to get far away from the person I had to be in the program. The day Josh wrote to me on Myspace, I'd been waiting for someone like him for months, an escape maybe, but also a grounding force to help me preserve a little bit of myself until I graduated. I could tolerate the costume I put on for school as long as I had something that was true at home.

Soon Josh and I were messaging each other every day. Other than him making the first move, he turned out to be shy. I didn't mind. It made him mysterious, and I had a healthy imagination to fill in the gaps. Gradually I pulled out of him that he was on his school's baseball team, that his favorite food was cafeteria pizza—details that I took to class and watered like seeds until they blossomed into visions of me cheering him on from the bleachers at his games, of wiping the tomato sauce from his mouth at lunch, while around me my classmates nodded along as Ms. Roth lectured us about crime scene safety. I knew I was getting a little carried away, but I didn't have a lot else going on.

A couple weeks of trading messages later, we exchanged numbers. I was self-conscious about my voice. My lisp. The way I sometimes accidentally pronounced parts of English words in Spanish. I brought the house phone into my room and nervously answered his questions about school, what I was wearing, trying to keep chill when he said I was easy to talk to. I told him about the mandatory afternoon drill trainings, getting yelled at in the blistering heat because I didn't salute correctly.

"Right now?" I said, staring down at the baggy T-shirt I always changed into when I got home. "Just boxers. What about you? What are you wearing?"

"You're making me blush," he said.

"Stop lying. No you're not!"

"I am. I haven't talked like this with anyone."

I could picture his lips on the other end of the line, his breath fogging up the receiver.

"Can I ask you something?" I said. "Does your family know?"

"No. They're . . . you know."

"Yeah," I said. "Mine neither."

The next day Josh called again. We couldn't hang out in real life—neither of us had cars, and where would two thirteen-year-olds go anyway?—but when we lay on our beds with our eyes closed and whispered, it was almost like we were in the same room next to each other.

Quickly, a routine formed: I'd get home from Boone. The phone would ring. I took it to my room, shut the door. What did we talk about? Movies, music, what we'd do in a zombie apocalypse. Sometimes we'd just breathe together for a while. At night, we'd fall asleep with our phones pressed to our ears, like kids with conch shells, listening to the oceans out of reach.

In December, the program took my class on a field trip to prison. A corrections officer funneled us through narrow hallways lined with glass-partitioned cells. Behind them, inmates smiled and called out to us, though we were strictly forbidden to speak back. As the officer giving us a tour walked ahead bragging about the shanks he'd confiscated that year, I saw that my boot-laces were undone. I bent down to tie them, when all of a sudden I heard nails tapping on glass above me. I raised my head. A foot from my face, an inmate stood in his cell holding a battered copy of *Maxim*. He lowered it, revealing his flaccid, wrinkled penis, his bushy pubes pointing in every direction like a thousand tiny question marks. I panicked and rushed to catch up with the group, anxiously wondering, *Why did he choose me? Did I stare too long? Could he tell I was gay?*

Back home, I picked up after one ring.

"Too bad. He can't have you!" Josh said once I was settled in bed. "You're mine."

"I am?" It'd been months since his first call. He'd never said anything like that.

"Yeah, dude."

"Totally." I hugged myself so it'd feel like he was holding me. "I wish I could see you. Like, see you for real. Not just pictures." I'd memorized all the ones on his Myspace. Josh at a birthday party, wearing that tight gray vest. At the beach, his soaking-wet basketball shorts clinging to his thighs. Now in my mind: Josh climbing on top of me. All his weight on me.

"This sucks." He sighed.

The sound of people laughing on his TV echoed in my receiver.

A week later I told him I was scared my mom knew about us. The prison field trip had made me more paranoid than usual.

Plus we were spending so much time on the phone. There was no way she hadn't noticed. Josh had the same concern. His parents were nosy, always in his business. Playing baseball got them off his back a little, he said. Could I do something like that?

"I don't know," I told him. "I'm not really sporty."

"You'll figure it out," he assured me. "You're smart. That's why I like you."

In the beginning, I tried to stay close to the truth. The whole point of Luis Lush was that, as him, I didn't have to pretend to be someone else. I confided in Josh about feeling suffocated every morning I stuffed myself into my uniform. How I was tired of having to act like I was straight but worried what would happen if I didn't. Gay people in the army were getting discharged for coming out—did he think something like that could happen to me in the program?

As the weeks passed, I sensed from his growing silences that he was losing interest in me, so I began to play with the facts I gave him, adding minor details to make myself seem more appealing. Yes, Boone was the worst, I told him, but my mom said she'd buy me a Range Rover if I didn't drop out. She works at the airport, I said vaguely, hoping he'd assume she was in management instead of a barista at Starbucks.

During a lull in another conversation, I casually dropped that I had an ex, an Abercrombie model, who wouldn't stop calling and messaging me.

"Desperate much?" I feigned annoyance into the phone, privately freaking out that I'd gone too far until he said, "What a weirdo, I'm sorry."

It would have been different if Josh and I were able to be

together in person. Then I could have gotten him to love my hand folded inside his, the feeling of our bodies sleeping side by side. Over the phone, I only had the idea of me to work with, the stories I could come up with. Lying gave me my body back. My power. Besides, if I had to lie to everyone I knew about being straight, I reasoned I should at least get to lie in a way that made me feel good. It was only fair.

That Christmas break, during the two-and-a-half-week vacation before classes started again in January, Mom sent Hector and me to visit Papi in Puerto Rico. I was excited to go, but also bummed that I wouldn't be able to talk to Josh for almost a month because Papi didn't have a computer and Mom lent us her phone for "emergencies only." No long distance.

It'd been a few years since I'd seen Papi. In the early days of the divorce, he flew in to visit us in Orlando a couple of times. He'd rent a room in whatever grimy, flea-infested motel he could afford by the airport, and we'd spend the week bingeing movies on the free cable, leaving only to go to the Waffle House or 7-Eleven or to take long, aimless drives with the windows down.

When he stopped coming, I tried not to blame him. He was far. Flights were expensive. And between our constant moving around, Mom's stroke, and it slowly dawning on me that I was gay, I had enough on my mind to keep from dwelling on his absence. That's not to say I didn't love him, but until we were reunited next, I placed him in the same mental drawer where I kept memories of pets that had run away: wherever he was, I just hoped he was okay.

On the plane ride to San Juan, I could barely contain myself. We were finally going to see him! There were so many things I needed to catch him up on! Omar being a jerk, always mad and stomping around the house and grunting at us—he should beat him up. Mom going back to work—how he should have been there to help her after the stroke.

As Hector and I walked off the plane, we watched all the other passengers who'd been on board with us hurry over to hug their waiting relatives. Their joyful reunions in perfect harmony with the Christmas music piping in through the airport speakers. We looked around for Papi's face in the crowd, but I couldn't find him anywhere. After a few minutes, my brother and I were the only ones left in the arrival terminal. Hector tried calling him, dialing over and over because the phone kept going to voicemail. "He forgot about us," I said. I grabbed the handle of my suitcase, flung myself down onto a nearby bench, and crossed my arms, feeling like an idiot.

An hour later I spotted a man walking quickly in our direction. He wore a ratty T-shirt, stretched out at the neck, and cargo shorts with a chain dangling off one of the belt loops. His brown skin was covered in pale splotches, some of them peeling at the edges, like moldy bread. It took me a minute before I recognized him. My father. In that moment it hit me that the rumors of his drug abuse weren't an exaggeration, like I'd told myself all my life. He looked like the men our teachers tried to scare us with at school. Mug shots. Faces tatted up. Florida men.

This could be you if you hit the pipe for five years. Everyone had laughed.

I leaped to my feet, swallowing my anger at his lateness, and ran over to him.

"¡Acho, pero guauuu!" Papi said, wrapping his scrawny arms around me and kissing the top of my head. His clothes stank of cheap cologne and cigarettes, nothing like Mom, but he was warm, and underneath his T-shirt I could hear his heart beating fast. I couldn't believe we were together. Hugging. Papi released me. "Look how big you are. You almost as tall as me."

I giggled maniacally.

"And you—" He took a step back, appraising Hector. "Damn, boy, you're grown now. How many girlfriends you got?" He gave him a friendly jab on the shoulder.

Hector smirked and scratched the back of his head. "Nothing serious."

"Uh-huh," Papi said. "I know what that means."

"How come you were late?" Hector asked. Of the two of us, he was the responsible one, the one who drove me to school in the morning in the janky Honda Civic he'd bought after getting a job at Old Navy, even though it made him tardy to his own special magnet high school.

"Oh, no, was I?" Papi said, looking to me for support.

I dropped my eyes to my shoes.

"Aw, man, I'm sorry." He grabbed the handles of both our suitcases. "Yeah, you're right. I'm late. You weren't here that long, were you? I'mma make it up to you, watch. I got this whole trip planned. I got my truck fixed up. We can camp on the beach, sleep under the stars. I'll take you to El Yunque. You remember El Yunque? I brought you when you were little. We're gonna have a good time, me and my boys. Christmas over here—phew, it's something else. You'll see."

Papi drove us to the house in Carolina where he was living with his adoptive mother, Titi Sixta, an Afro–Puerto Rican woman who'd taken him in as a baby after his mom abandoned him to deal with her own substance abuse issues. For most of the first week, Papi either napped or left us with Titi while he disappeared for hours, claiming he was going out "for a drive," not returning until late in the night, when he'd stumble into our room and curl up on the floor.

One morning he told us to pack our bags and took us to stay at a house that a friend of his was supposedly lending him. Papi said his friend had gone on vacation, but most of the lights didn't work, and we'd had to open the bedroom door with a hanger. I asked Hector if he thought we'd broken in, but he said no, that was silly, our dad wasn't *that* messed up. Papi bought us a giant tin of saltines and a smoked sausage to make sandwiches while he was out, which was still most of the time. With nothing to do, my brother and I stayed in bed bored, sweating through our dirty clothes waiting for him to return. On Christmas, we went back to Titi's, who was clearly annoyed with Papi for not making any effort and compensated by stuffing us with pasteles and letting us sit in front of the TV all day.

The trip passed by in a dull fog. We didn't do any of the things he'd promised. We probably spent more meaningful time together at the airport.

I didn't know what to think. I'd missed my dad, his cooking, the way he could make me feel like there were no rules, sleeping in till two p.m. when we lived together in Miami, egging me on when I'd throw a towel on my head and lip-sync to Britney Spears. Yet in Puerto Rico, when he'd leave us to go on his drives, I found myself relieved, because just the sight of my father underscored what had begun to feel inevitable since we'd reunited: that unless I did something, I would end up like him, in and out of jail, homeless in spurts. A disappointment.

Our family always said I took after him: the same curly hair, same scrunched-up brown eyes. During his naps, I studied him, fearing there might be deeper similarities between us too. By then, I'd internalized the lessons that the program had taught me about addicts: that their problems were individual, of their own creation and thus their own fault, and the best solution was to lock them up and throw away the key. I needed to believe he'd made a choice to be this way, so in turn I could choose to be different. When the trip ended, anticlimactically, I was happy to put some distance between us again. Or maybe that's just what I told myself, since he seemed to be perfectly happy without us. It'd be fifteen years before I saw my father again.

Back from PR, I came up with a plan to finally meet Josh, a real man. Every Friday morning, freshmen in the program were required to go to the criminal justice homeroom, where the older grades baked hundreds of chocolate chip cookies for us to sell to our classmates. It was how we fundraised for the "free" trip to Washington seniors took every year—after four years of selling cookies, we earned enough to pay our way. We were supposed to take ten bags of cookies from a large bin that was set out for us and sell them for a dollar each, but once I noticed there was no one really monitoring how many cookies we took, I saw a chance to take extra bags and pocket the change. I could make ten, fifteen bucks a week that way.

My goal was to save enough money for a date. I wanted to take Josh someplace good. I needed to keep up with the lies I told him. At first I'd only implied that Mom had an impressive job, but over time I'd fabricated an elaborate story that our family was in the citrus industry and were heirs to an orange fortune and had several luxury cars and houses. I apologized for not telling him, claiming people judged us for being rich, treated us different when they found out.

"I'm sorry. I just want to be normal," I told him.

"No, you don't," Josh said. "Trust me. You don't know how lucky you are."

Halfway through the year, I'd made one friend at Boone. Colton. We met in French class, the one hour of the school day when I was required to speak. I sat behind him in class, admiring his long blond hair and the ease with which he got along with everybody: the drama kids and football players, the stoners who gathered in circles at lunch to play hacky sack. Colton was a skateboarder, which made him a little bit of everything, I guess. Theatrical. Athletic. Goofy.

We were mostly acquaintances until one afternoon, he saw me across the street from Boone, waiting for Hector to pick me up, and asked if I wanted to come over sometime. He said he could teach me to skateboard. I didn't really want to. I didn't have a board. But he offered to give me his old one, so I accepted the invitation, thinking it might help throw Mom off my scent if she saw me hanging out with a straight boy instead of glued to the TV watching *America's Next Top Model*. And I figured she'd make an exception to the "no going to other kids' houses" rule, since the alternative was moping around campus for the hour it took Hector to come get me.

The following day I rode the school bus with Colton to his house. I had imagined, from his raggedy clothes and bony arms, that his family was middle-class at best, so I was surprised when the bus dropped us off at the entrance to a gated community full of McMansions. We walked side by side through his neighborhood while I discreetly observed the manicured lawns and model-year cars parked in driveways, not a single broken bottle or pothole in the road.

His house was one of the largest. All the furniture was white or off-white, and there were fresh flowers everywhere. His parents owned their own business, he'd later tell me with a casual shrug, like that was their job: business. We headed straight into the farmhouse-style kitchen, where everything was bathed in the soft, ethereal light filtering in through a set of bay windows by their breakfast nook. I tried to act unfazed, taking in the LIVE LOVE LAUGH sign carved out of bleached wood hanging over the oven. God, it was fabulous.

But what stunned me most were the snacks. The kitchen cabinets had glass doors, and behind them were family-size bags of Doritos, Lay's, tubs of peanut butter and granola. Enough food to survive an apocalypse. At my house, if I got hungry between meals, I took a nap.

I smiled at Colton, like *Yes, of course, this is how I live too! Living, loving, laughing!*

"Gimme a second," he said, dropping his bag on the floor and bouncing out of the kitchen. "Gotta pee—be right back! Help yourself to anything!"

I knew better than to actually help myself to anything at somebody else's house. Just out of curiosity, though, as soon as he was out of the room I stepped closer to the cabinets to see what else they had. I was standing there, my mouth watering over a bag of chocolate-covered pretzels, when suddenly I felt something cold and hard tickle the back of my neck. Colton's pale face reflected on the glass door. I turned around, still smiling. "Hey, are you getting—" I started to ask.

"Don't move," he cut me off once I was facing him.

That's when I saw it. What he'd poked me with. A gun. A long, skinny one, the hunting kind. He rammed it into my chest.

"Wh—" I stuttered. "Wh—what is that? What are you doing?"

I put my hands up, pressing my back up against the counter.

"Shut up." He smirked, pleased by my reaction. My eyes darted from his face to the trigger to the barrel, but that was worse. The dark hole at the end. Threatening to swallow me.

"This isn't funny," I said. My hands trembled in the air. "I don't like this."

"Bitch, I'm going to kill you," he cackled.

"Colton," I said as calmly as I could. "For real, stop." I thought about running, but what if my moving scared him and he shot me? "Colton," I pleaded, shaking, "please."

41

He parroted my voice back like I was a whiny baby. "'Colton stoooop. Colton plleeeeaseee. I don't like this!'"

I stared him directly in the eye, ready to beg. "Colton. Come on. Put it down."

He stared back at me for a long while. His nostrils twitched, then a wide, toothy grin spread across his face. "Damn, I was just kidding!" He lowered the gun. "Were you scared?"

I waited for him to put the gun on the counter. Then I slapped the shit out of him.

"What the FUCK is wrong with you?" I exploded. "Don't you EVER point a fucking gun at me. Do you understand? Don't you EVER fucking do that, you fucking PSYCHO!" My chest deflated, like I was releasing all the rage I had trapped inside me. "Fuck you, you fucking asshole."

Colton blinked. When he opened his eyes again, they were glossed over. A tear crawled down his cheek where my pink handprint bloomed. "I'm sorry," he said, and looked away.

It'd been less than five minutes since I'd come over. The knowledge of that pounded in every cell of my body, followed by the realization that Hector wouldn't pick me up for another half hour, that Mom would have a panic attack if I told her any of this, that I was alone in a neighborhood where I didn't know anybody, and that I had made some white boy cry.

"It's . . . okay," I sighed. "Just don't do that again."

More tears fell from his eyes, but he stayed quiet.

"I'm sorry, too," I added. "It's just that you . . . I—I was . . . You all right?"

He nodded.

We stood there in awkward silence while a clock nearby loudly marked the seconds.

"So," I said.

Colton wiped his face. "Wanna go to my room?" he spoke up at last.

I let out a deep breath. "Okay."

He turned around and ran out of the kitchen, up a flight of stairs. I followed behind him, privately counting the minutes left until Hector came to take me home.

Colton's bedroom was huge, bigger than Mom's, the walls covered with posters of Tony Hawk and Biggie. Next to a fish tank was a desk with his own Apple computer. He rushed over to his bed, dropped to his knees, and pulled out a shoebox from beneath the bed frame, removing the lid to retrieve a Ziploc bag. I could see a lighter and a couple of loosely wrapped joints inside, the weed spilling out through cracks in the paper.

"You smoke?" He held a joint toward me like an olive branch.

"When do your parents get home?" I asked, taking it. I'd only smoked once before. A cousin's weed years earlier. I remembered how nice it was, my brain shutting off for a while.

"Don't worry about it," he said. "Not till late."

I felt kind of bad for him, how someone could have so much and no one at the same time. That had to be lonely. I slumped down onto the carpet and reached for the lighter.

By the end of January, I had saved enough from selling cookies to take Josh out. We'd been together almost four months at that point, and as the weeks passed, I'd been dropping more and more hints about wanting to see him, that I didn't have Valentine's Day plans yet, and Hector would probably be able to pick us up and take us somewhere if we pretended to be friends. I'd mostly gotten over Colton's "joke" from the day I went over—he did seem genuinely sorry afterward—but still, ever since that afternoon, I hadn't been able to get out of my head that if he had accidentally shot me, I would have died without having done anything with my life, nothing compared to Luis Lush. I'd never even kissed someone. But I was going to change that.

Then one day Josh called.

"Are you alone?" he asked, dread thick in his voice.

Mom was sleeping; Hector at work at Old Navy. I took the phone into my room and sat on my bed, bracing myself for him to tell me he was moving or some other bad news.

"Yeah?" I said. "Why?"

"The FBI is recording us," he blurted out.

I laughed. "What?"

"I'm serious," he said. "My dad's an agent. I know, it's a lot. I wasn't allowed to tell anyone, but I just found out they monitor their employees' calls. *Shhh,* listen."

I obeyed and held my breath, pressing my ear tightly to my phone's receiver. Even to me the whole thing sounded crazy. As if the government would waste money surveilling teenagers. At the same time, I didn't want it to be a lie. Partly because it made me feel special, like our affair was a matter of national security, like we were Marilyn Monroe and JFK, not two sad, closeted losers in Orlando. But also because Josh had told me so little about himself. His favorite color: "Blue?" he'd mumbled during our first phone call. I thought it was sweet he was nervous. Where he lived: "Near downtown. Sorry, can't say where." It had taken months to get him to start opening up to me. If I doubted him now, I could scare him away.

I waited to hear something. The line was silent. Nothing. Not a single sound. That didn't stop me from picturing a man wearing headphones driving up and down the street in a white van, trying to pinpoint my exact location. I stood up and went to my bedroom window, squinting past the cracked glass to the road in front of the house. There wasn't anyone out there.

Of course not.

I sat back down on my bed, scolding myself for being so gullible.

Just as I was about to ask Josh what was going on, there was a noise on the other end of the line. It might have been an exhale, or a phone briefly sliding down a cheek. Whatever it was, it lasted less than a second, but it was there. Fuck. The FBI *was* spying on us. Thank God.

"You heard that?" Josh said.

I dropped my voice to a whisper. "I think so. Yeah."

"Told you. We have to be careful. Okay?"

"Yeah," I said. "Okay."

After that, we returned to Myspace. It'd be safer, Josh said. The FBI was only keeping tabs on his dad's calls as standard protocol, but if someone found out about us, it's possible they'd tell him. It would be better if we didn't get together for a while either, just in case. Some days Josh sent me a short message. *Miss you. Thinking of you.* Others he didn't write anything.

I didn't worry. This was temporary. More time to save up for our first date.

Valentine's Day came and went. I slept with my legs wrapped around my pillow.

Maybe if it were happening to a friend, I would have been able to see all the red flags. If the FBI were tapping my phone, wouldn't they have heard him warning me? And why couldn't he write more than a couple of sentences? I wasn't dumb, but I was in love, which does take a certain amount of willful ignorance. Josh was the first person I'd ever told I was gay. In the whirlwind of my admission, I needed him to be telling me the truth, or else it would mean I was stupid for putting my defenses down. It would mean that after everything I had made up about how rich and cool and wanted I was, it still wasn't enough for him to want me.

Anyway, he couldn't be lying. I was the liar.

Without Josh's calls to come home to, I started spending more time after school with Colton. He didn't care that I didn't speak much or that I was terrible at skateboarding. I was too afraid of taking risks, like he did, riding his skateboard off of stairwells, trying to grind on rails. Every time we got stoned in his bedroom and watched skating videos where teenage boys broke their legs and cracked open their skulls trying to one-up each other, all I could think of was what would happen to me if I got hurt, what Mom would do with another hospital bill.

Mostly we skated in the parking lot at the mall. Colton kept his word and gave me his old board. But he also gave me old clothes of his, too. T-shirts he didn't wear anymore. Sneakers. I was embarrassed when he offered. It reminded me of the Christmas a social worker gave Hector and me presents in a garbage bag and how we had to feign gratitude and say "thank you!" for a useless hockey kit in *Florida* while this lady clutched her heart like she was going to cry.

But the bag Colton handed me was good, full of brand names. Volcom. KR3W. I'd been dying to own a pair of skinny jeans, and here was a pair with the tag still on that he claimed didn't fit him anymore. "Oh," I said, downplaying my excitement. "Cool, thanks." When we were tired of skating, we'd climb up the small hill behind the mall and lie on the soft grass, using our boards as pillows as we smoked his weed and watched the clouds slowly roll by.

Once, when we were lying there taking a break beneath a shady tree, he turned to me and asked, "Do you think I'm ugly?"

I looked at him from the corner of my eye. "What? Why?"

In my head, I went over his features. Wavy blond hair, freckles, bruises on his arms. I wasn't attracted to him, but some days I wondered what it'd be like to try out his face for a while.

"I asked this girl out, and she . . .," Colton said, then frowned a little and sat up. "Whatever. Come here." He took a long, hard puff from the joint in his hand and patted his lap.

I got on my knees and crawled over. When I was in front of him, he grabbed the back of my head roughly, curled his lips so they looked like the barrel of a gun, and pulled me in until our noses were touching. A plume of smoke trailed out of his mouth and slipped into mine.

"Shotgun!" He exhaled, coughing.

As his hands let go of my hair, my dick hardened against the inside of my jeans. I didn't know if it was him, or that my lips had been so close to a boy's. I suppose there wasn't much of a difference. I swallowed and coughed too, arranging my board over my legs.

"You're not ugly," I said.

A strange expression flashed across Colton's face. I couldn't tell what he was thinking, whether he saw me. He was difficult to read, and my vision was blurring.

"Thanks." He smiled. "You don't really count, though, right?"

It felt like an opening, like he was daring me to say something. For a second I imagined us rolling around on the grass, making out like any other couple. Would he want that? Did I?

I lay back down again, wishing I was with Josh. "Yeah. Right," I said. "I don't."

Just a few months before the end of the school year, Colton started selling weed on campus. Not a lot, it seemed. Dime bags to his friends, acquaintances. I didn't get why. His parents could buy him anything he wanted. I thought it was weird, bored rich kid behavior, but I didn't tell him that. It wasn't any of my business, and who was I to question him when he'd been so generous, giving me the clothes off his back and smoking me out several times a week?

Because I was in the program and he took regular classes, we were hardly ever together at Boone anyway other than when we walked to French for the last period of the day. Usually we kept to ourselves on the way to class, but the more money he earned dealing, the cockier he became, waving baggies in the air, yelling, "Yooo, I got weed! Who wants some?"

It was mortifying. I said *what the hell are you doing, stop being crazy, this is embarrassing, you're gonna get caught,* but he just laughed and mimicked me with the same whiny voice he'd used in his kitchen—"Colton stoppp! Colton put that away! That's not funnyyyy!"—like this was one of his dumb jokes.

When I realized everything I said only egged him on, I began to linger a few steps behind him on our walks. I figured he was going through a phase and that it would pass eventually. In the meantime, if Colton wanted to act like a clown, whatever, that was on him.

I should've stopped hanging out with him, but I wasn't in any position to throw away a friend, and I'd gotten hooked to his gifts, his weed, to his parents chauffeuring us to the skate park and the mall, whereas Mom didn't have the energy to leave the house most of the time. Plus he wasn't as annoying when we were alone. And out of everyone else, he'd chosen me. So after the final bell rang, I continued riding the bus to his place. We climbed up the stairs to his room, played Tony Hawk, raided his pantry. Normal teenager things. I guess I didn't want to give that up either.

One morning I woke up early to message Josh before school. He'd been a little more distant than usual, and I wanted to ask if everything was okay, whether he was still interested in meeting. When I opened my inbox, I saw that he'd changed his profile picture to a plain gray square. I clicked through to his page, confused. Myspace directed me to an error report:

This user has deleted their account.

I stared at it for a minute, my mouse cursor drowning in the white screen.

I considered calling his house, but he'd explicitly told me not to. His school, but I didn't know where he went, and what would I even say? I didn't know much about him, only that he lived "near downtown," that he liked bad cafeteria pizza, and that his dad worked for the FBI. I'd believed him when he first told me, but as I sat there, realizing I had no way to reach him, the ridiculousness of that lie sank in. The FBI? Seriously? He probably just wanted to get rid of me and didn't want to say it. There was no one I could talk to without revealing my secret, no one to help me understand why my chest felt hard, but I couldn't cry. Was this even a loss? We'd never gotten together, kissed, held hands. Nothing. Can you lose something you never really had?

That day I moved on the way the program had prepared me to: I put on my cargo pants, laced up my boots, and went to school in a numb daze. No one noticed anything wrong with me, because I didn't give them anything to notice. For once, I was grateful boys didn't have to have feelings.

We were in the middle of criminal justice class when someone knocked on the door. A hush fell over the room. Ms. Roth paused her lecture, clearly irritated, and went to see who it was, her shoulders relaxing at the sight of the officer's dark blue uniform. Their conversation was too low to eavesdrop on from my seat in the back row, but I could tell they were talking about me, because her eyes kept darting from his face to mine. When he finished speaking, she called out my name. "Edgar!" I gaped around at my classmates, at the boy who'd asked if I was in a gang. They were all staring back at me. "Oooooh, you're in trouble," I heard someone say.

"Enough," Ms. Roth said. "Edgar, I need you to go with him. Now."

I looked down at the composition book I'd been taking notes in. There was a test coming up, and I'd been determined to do well on it. Since Josh disappeared, I'd focused all my attention on getting good grades. All I cared about was qualifying for a college scholarship so once I graduated I'd be able to do whatever I wanted. As long as I kept my mind on the future, I didn't have to think about how right now I was alone. Venn diagrams filled the pages of my composition book, words double- and triple-underlined. I hadn't finished copying the latest slide projected on the board, my notes abruptly cutting off at the moment when the officer knocked on the door.

"Do I take my stuff?" I asked.

"Yes," the officer answered for her.

I took my time, slowly sliding my notebook into my backpack while I tried to figure out what this could be about. Had something happened to Mom? No, she'd been doing a lot better lately. Did they know I'd been stealing cookies? Shit, what if I gave the money back?

I got up and followed the officer out of the classroom. We walked together silently to the opposite end of campus until we reached a low, one-story building I hadn't been to before. Once inside, we went down a narrow hallway. At the end of it was a dimly lit room with a small metallic table. Ice-cold air coughed out of the overhead vents. The officer escorted me in.

"Sit down," he said, taking a seat himself.

I did like he said.

"Do you know why you're here?"

"No." I set my backpack by my feet. "Why?"

He leaned in. "We've been monitoring you."

I scanned my peripheral vision. What was he talking about? Who was *we*?

"We know what you've been doing," the officer went on.

Know what you've been doing. Monitoring you. He sounded like Josh. I didn't have time for this. I had to get back to class.

"You and your friend."

He slid an ID across the table. Colton's pale face smiled up at me.

I brought my hands down to my lap and picked at my fingernails.

The officer told me they'd been keeping tabs on us for weeks, that they had "photographic evidence" of our "drug deals." He said they had caught a girl with marijuana, and she'd named Colton, and he'd named me, so I shouldn't bother denying it, because they'd already interviewed him and he'd confirmed that I was his accomplice.

As he spoke, I could feel his cold glare dissecting me, as if he were seeking more evidence of my crimes in my appearance. I lowered my eyes and saw a drop of blood blooming where I'd picked my nail too hard. I wrapped my other hand around it, feeling my pulse racing against my palm. The room shrank, the walls closing in on me. Why would Colton say I was an accomplice? Where was he? I'd never sold weed. If anything, I'd practically begged him to stop.

The officer kept talking, but I wasn't able to connect the words coming out of his mouth to the me sitting in front of him. It was like he was talking about someone else, someone who looked like me and had the same name, and this other me disgusted him. This other me was bad, a drug dealer. Corrupting all the poor innocent kids at Boone. And though I knew I hadn't been his accomplice, I also thought: I *did* smoke with Colton. If they tested me, they'd find that.

If I wanted this to be over, the officer told me, I had to give him a written statement. He pushed a sheet of paper toward me, next to Colton's ID.

"Don't make this harder on yourself. The easier you make this for us, the less trouble you'll be in." He held out a pencil, his voice turning friendly. "Don't you want to go?"

Go? I wasn't sure what he meant. Could I just leave? Getting to go sounded nice. I wanted to go home, to go to bed and wake up from a long sleep with the past year erased from my memory. Papi's moldy skin. Colton's gun. Josh on the phone, telling me I was his. I wanted my mom.

I took the pencil and stared down at the blank sheet of paper.

"My name is Edgar Gomez," I began to write, then froze, not sure what to put next.

"Come on," the officer said. "It won't be as bad for you if you tell the truth."

The *truth?* I weighed the word in my mind.

He already seemed to have decided what the truth was. He said he had pictures, I assumed of Colton walking to class with me lurking behind him. He said I could go.

I brought the pencil back down to the paper. Wrote that yes, I was Colton's accomplice. Because I couldn't think of any other way out of that office than to lie. Because I believed him when he said the consequences wouldn't be as terrible for me if I gave him a statement confessing what I'd done. So I tried to do that as convincingly as I could, writing through tears about my crimes, how I'd been smoking for years, probably got it from my father, that I was friends with whoever the girl was, sprinkling in extra details like that I had weed in my backpack and in my locker. The officer didn't send someone to check, or ask for my bag to confiscate the drugs that were supposedly the reason I was there. If he had, he would've seen I'd made it up.

It would become the official record of my story on file. By the end of the day, I'd be expelled from Boone and the criminal justice program. Colton would be expelled too. His parents would enroll him at an expensive private Catholic school, and I'd be sent to Oak Ridge, the school that I was zoned for from the start. I would never speak to Colton again, but for a few months, I would follow him on Myspace, becoming more and more bitter as he posted pictures of his fun field trips and new friends, as if the expulsion had somehow improved his life. And I'd wonder if he ever thought of me, whether he knew what would happen when he said my name.

But while I was still in the office, writing my statement, what got me more than anything was how good I was at pretending, a practiced liar. A small part of me even enjoyed it, like I was telling an entertaining story and the officer would be proud of me for my honesty and cooperation. When I finished, I wiped my eyes and pushed the paper back.

The officer glanced through it quickly once, shook his head, and filed it away without saying a word. My story did not amuse him. He was not surprised. This had all been written before.

3

FAKE

Junior year of high school, my mom took me to the dentist to have my teeth filed down into sharp, flat daggers, then covered with perfect, shinier teeth, like press-on nails. They were called veneers. All the Hollywood It Girls like Hilary Duff were getting them at the time, whereas my broke-ass classmates could barely afford fake vampire teeth for their Halloween costumes.

Technically, Mom couldn't afford to buy me veneers either. Once as a kid, I asked her if she could take me to the library, and she told me we couldn't go because gas was too expensive. It wasn't the first time I realized we were poor, but it was the first time our poverty seemed cartoonishly inescapable: we couldn't even afford to drive five blocks for free shit.

I'd been obsessed with my teeth since the fifth grade, when being gap-toothed stopped being cute, and the kids with naturally straight teeth started pairing off to preserve their superior evolutionary lines. My teeth weren't *endearingly* bad. I'm not talking about a tiny gap I could rebrand as *quirky*. Some of them were missing, the rest looked like rotting toenails. There was one stubborn baby tooth at the very front of my mouth that refused to fall off no matter how hard I tugged at it. I watched in horror well into my teenage years as all my other teeth began to crowd around it, strangling each other, fighting for air. I brushed them as soon as I woke up, after every meal, plus two or three times in between, to be safe. I thought making them whiter would distract from how awful they were, but after almost a decade of fanatical brushing, all that happened was my gumline receded. Google said I might even need gum surgery. Surgery!

I'd been bugging my mom for years about braces. During a trip we took to Nicaragua to visit relatives, I practically dragged her to a dentist, who said he could put some on me for cheap, but there was no way to get around having to fly back every few months to get them adjusted. I promised I would figure out a way to pay for the plane tickets myself, that the second we were back in Orlando, I would get a job and save every penny.

Still: "I'm sorry," she said. "Maybe next year."

But a year might as well have been an eternity, and I understood perfectly what she meant by "maybe." I told her not to worry about it and stayed quiet the rest of the afternoon, brooding out of the car window on the drive home.

By the time I made it to high school, I'd added my teeth to

the growing list of things I hoped would simply resolve them-selves in the future: being gay, my acne, whatever mental illness I had that compelled me to stay up all night watching rom-coms and biting my nails until they bled. It was easier to tell myself that adult me would find solutions to these problems than to fixate on what I couldn't change in the moment. For a while, this strategy worked.

Then I was expelled from the criminal justice program on drug charges, and suddenly the future became just as unreli-able as the present. I spent the summer between getting kicked out of Boone and starting at my new school, Oak Ridge, pacing my bedroom, spiraling. What if the expulsion stopped me from getting into college? Would adult me still be able to get a good job, or at least one with dental insurance? What if my smile al-ways made people cringe? Who could love someone like that? Broke, with fucked-up teeth. What now? I used to think I was smart. Used to think that was something. But I was wrong. What was I supposed to do now?

My mom was the first person to teach me the importance of being beautiful. Ever since I was a child, she kept our fridge stocked with homemade creams she'd concocted by blending aloe and avocados from our yard. She'd lock herself in the bath-room once a month and emerge with her hair tinted a slightly different shade of red: Radiant Ruby, Cinnamon Sensation, whatever was on sale at Sally Beauty Supply. She wouldn't leave the house without applying lipstick, mascara, blush, and her signature smoky purple eye shadow, or without high heels on, which she swore she was more comfortable in than flats. She lived for press-on nails and leopard print, for people to smell her perfume before she entered a room. At home, she walked around with her breasts hanging out and peed with the door wide open. Mom was proud of her body.

But she also had a pair of flippers, those creepy, removable fake teeth they make little girls wear in beauty pageants to look like dolls. She'd bought them for a hundred or so dollars in Nica and only took them off at night, keeping them in a Starbucks mug by her bed, ready for her the second she woke up. I know a part of her remembered what it was like to have bad teeth, because it was still evident in all the small mannerisms we shared. The way we pressed our lips tight in pictures. How we instinctively covered our mouths with the back of our hands when we laughed. Mom knew how it felt being afraid to smile, and the impact that had on everything else.

That isn't what changed her mind about fixing my teeth, though. What was different, the year she finally took me to a dentist in Orlando, was that she was declaring bankruptcy. In the early 2000s, it seemed everyone was. The country was scrambling to get back on its feet after the recession. For years, banks moved in the shadow of the crumbling economy, offering predatory loans like the one Mom received to buy our house, trapping her in an endless payment cycle during which she could hardly cover the interest. Desperate for help, she'd called the number of a lawyer she saw on a billboard who said a bankruptcy would give her a fresh start and wipe out the mountain of credit card debt that had been accumulating since she divorced Papi.

What he didn't say, but she must have inferred, was that it was also her chance to make one last big purchase.

I was only vaguely aware of the bankruptcy the day Mom drove me to the dentist. Part of me was convinced she was taking me just so I'd get off her back, and once we arrived at the clinic, she'd tell me no again, like in Nicaragua. I was sixteen by then—skeptical of anything trying to pass itself off as good news. This clinic was too nice for people like us, I thought, taking a seat in the waiting room. Portraits of happy blond families hung on the walls, their cruel white smiles beaming down at me as elevator jazz piped in from hidden speakers.

When the dentist, Dr. Franklin, emerged through a door and called out my name, I slid lower in my seat. He was younger than I'd expected, dressed like a former jock in a button-up shirt rolled up to his muscular biceps, and we were about to waste an hour of his time discussing my biggest insecurity. Mom forced me up by the arm. We followed Dr. Franklin to a screened-off room, where he instructed me to lie down and open my mouth wide so he could inspect inside with little silver tools. Just in case I'd ever deluded myself into thinking my teeth weren't that bad, he began to list their various flaws: crooked, not enough room, growing inward.

"No cavities, though," he said, sounding surprised. "Good for you."

I lay there, trying not to choke on my own saliva.

In the end, Dr. Franklin gave Mom the same monologue I'd already heard from the last dentist. Braces weren't a one-and-done thing. In my case, they required a minimum two-year commitment. He rattled off prices I didn't bother paying attention to.

I would have preferred he slapped me on the face; it would've been less humiliating than pretending to take him seriously.

I was preparing for us to go when, out of nowhere, Mom asked about alternatives to braces. My ears perked up. What was this about? So did Dr. Franklin's, because he reappraised us, as if trying to fit a newly discovered piece into an already complete puzzle. My dirty sneakers. Mom's bamboo earrings. He shifted in his chair, then mentioned that a popular new option was veneers, but it was a more extreme route that most clients found too expensive for—

"That's fine," Mom cut him off sharply.

I looked at her sideways from the bed. *That's fine? Fine for who?* Where was the lady who bought underwear by the Ziploc bag at the flea market?

Dr. Franklin nodded apologetically and went on to say that I was an excellent candidate. Because my baby tooth had never fallen off, after removing it there would be a large space in my smile that would take years for the braces to correct, but veneers could cover that problem area up instantly. In fact, he said, he could do some X-rays, order the veneers, and give me a brand-new smile all within a month. The veneers were $900 per tooth, plus installment fees. About $16,000 in total.

It was Mom who shifted in her chair now. She lowered her eyes and bit her lip, trying to calculate how much credit she had between her cards.

"What if we do just the top half of his teeth?" she asked after a while, lifting her eyes to Dr. Franklin again. "Those are the only ones people can see anyway, right?"

He cleared his throat. "Yes," he said. "That's . . . possible."

The total would come out closer to $8,000, but I wouldn't need to return for readjustments, as with braces.

"Okay," Mom said. "What do we have to do?"

When Dr. Franklin's assistant marched over in a pair of Minnie Mouse Crocs to hand Mom the paperwork, I felt dizzy with disbelief, as if I'd stepped into the most incredible movie and none of the actors had realized I had locked the actual star, a spoiled little rich boy who casually did rich people shit like get veneers, into his trailer and taken his place. I didn't dare speak or move, worried the wrong action on my part would alert the cast and bring the film to a screeching halt.

Mom, swiping several credit cards before signing on the dotted line.

Dr. Franklin, shaking my flabby hand, kindly ignoring the sweat gathered there.

His assistant, guiding me to a blank wall, an explosion of light as she took the Polaroid she explained would be used as my Before picture.

A few minutes later I found myself in a cozy, dimly lit office, where she placed in front of me a ruler-sized slab of wood with a dozen teeth glued to it, side by side, in shades ranging from Beige to Pastor at Megachurch. It looked like something she'd fished out of a radioactive swamp.

"Which color you want for your veneers, hun?" she asked.

I was so close to getting away with it. I hesitated, wondering whether this was one last test. It didn't made sense—what idiot would pick a shade other than the whitest? Surely no one would be so tragic as to settle for mediocrity when they could be great? But even if it was a test, Mom had a receipt in her bag and a date set. There was nothing stopping us now. I pointed at the best tooth, at the end of the slab, imagining it in my mouth and the doors it would open. With a full set like that, I could get any job, date anyone I wanted. Images of myself as a doctor or a lawyer flashed behind my eyes, clinking wineglasses with my husband in our tasteful brownstone in Manhattan, the two of us cracking up about the time I got kicked out of school and thought I'd ruined my future. I felt an awkward pull in my cheeks, the muscles contracting in a way I wasn't used to. I couldn't help it. I was smiling.

"This one!" I practically cackled.

"No." The assistant frowned. "You don't want that one. It's too white for you. Trust me. Choose one with a little yellow, or no one is going to believe they're real."

Since starting at Oak Ridge, I'd mostly minded my business, trying to focus on my grades and prove to Mom I wasn't a complete mess. The memory of the afternoon I came home from Boone and told her I'd gotten expelled still haunted me. I'd anticipated tears, a fight. She was not one of those chill American parents who let stuff slide. Energy drinks were drugs to her. Walking around the house barefoot: a war crime. But she'd listened to me tell her about my failure in silence, didn't even flinch when I mentioned the marijuana charges. That crushed me more than the expulsion itself. It was like she expected me to disappoint her. I was Papi's kid, right?

More confusing than her nonreaction was that, after the initial shock started wearing off, I felt relieved to be free of Boone and the criminal justice program. I didn't miss the teachers who monitored the length of my hair down to the centimeter, the weeks I hadn't spoken a word. Maybe the recruiter who'd convinced me to apply to the program was a liar, and it wasn't the worst thing to go to Oak Ridge. Walking through the hallways on campus, I'd pass my predominantly Puerto Rican and Haitian classmates gossiping in Spanish and Creole, hanging out by their lockers munching on bags of cereal. Being around teenagers who looked and sounded like me was like letting go of a deep breath I hadn't noticed I was keeping in. It was like going to school with a bunch of cousins. We just *got* each other.

Another bonus: as the new kid, I was a novelty. In the early days, students in class all climbed over each other to be my friend. Did I play sports? they asked. Have a girlfriend? Could I sit next to them? The kindness they welcomed me with helped me bring down the walls I'd built around myself at Boone. They confirmed that Oak Ridge was where I'd always belonged.

A few months in, riding on the wave of my popularity, I told a boy I was gay. We were at the bus stop waiting to be picked up. Something about the way Angel sat, with one leg tucked under his butt, made me feel like he wouldn't be weirded out. And he was in drama club, so there was that.

The gold cross around his neck glinted in the sunlight. "I think I am too," Angel said.

Everything happened quickly, like we'd both been starving before we showed up in each other's lives. By the next day, we were boyfriends. Making out behind the theater at the far end of campus, me on my tiptoes to get on his level. Switching hoodies between periods while our teachers shook their heads. I was so smitten that I had a boo I could touch and kiss and text good morning and goodnight to that it didn't bother me that my reputation around school was changing.

Being out wasn't the automatic death sentence it'd been in the past, but it wasn't anything to be celebrated either. These were the days of *Mean Girls,* of Christina Aguilera wailing *You are beautifullll* on the radio, and yet a common argument on every morning talk show was that if gays were given the right to marry, next people would start marrying their dogs. My straight classmates didn't know what to do with me. Initially they followed the script their parents must have in the '80s, their questions turning from curious to accusatory. How did I know I didn't like pussy if I hadn't tried it? What did I do about all the shit when I had sex? Did one of my uncles *touch* me? Nothing I hadn't heard in some corny after-school special. But it was like they also understood how tired those jokes were, and gradually their disgust faded into ambivalence.

Caught up in the excitement of being in love, I shrugged at the warning signs: how Angel and I only kissed in hiding, the worn Bible he carried around in his backpack. When we broke up—he made a mistake, Angel said, a phase, he told people—I was suddenly aware of how compromised I'd become. I was okay with him by my side, but now I was out on my own, my loneliness multiplied by my classmates' avoidance of me.

One boy who I'd been eating lunch with found out I'd tried to "turn" Angel gay and said we couldn't be seen together. He said he'd made real friends he'd be having lunch with.

The Gay Kid was irrelevant in the grand scheme of things, after all, not *real* friend material, not worthy of sharing meals with and too pathetic to even enjoy bullying anymore. The same classmates who'd wanted to know me when I was new had long ago backed away. Their offer of community, just as I began to believe I deserved one, withdrawn. I took their rejection as another expulsion, except worse: I never expected anything from kids at Boone. But at Oak Ridge, I'd started to think I could be someone. At lunch, I went to the library, laid my head down at an empty table, and pretended to sleep as the cheerful din of students eating outside echoed in my ears. I did that for a year.

The day of the procedure, Mom picked me up from school right after she got off work. We arrived at the dentist's office twenty minutes early and parked under a shady tree. While we waited, Mom pulled a thin cardigan out of her purse, buttoned it over the green Starbucks mermaid sewn onto her uniform, then lowered the driver's seat mirror to dab concealer under her eyes and apply a fresh coat of mascara. She must have been exhausted.

"Ready?" she asked.

I leaped over the divider and wrapped my arms tight around her chest.

"Thank you," I whispered.

She kissed the top of my head. "You're welcome. Now you can't say I don't love you."

Before he began, Dr. Franklin gave Mom and me a lecture on upkeep. There were hard foods I'd need to avoid for the rest of my life: no apples, no candy. And I shouldn't try opening bottles with my veneers, he winked. I nodded politely, as if any of those things mattered to me. I would have given him my soul. He said the veneers were made to last about ten years, though with proper care they could last up to fifteen, and then I'd have to replace them.

That, actually, gave me pause. It meant there'd come a day when I'd need to come up with $8,000, an impossible sum of money, nearly half what Mom made in an entire year. Yet I also knew that once I had veneers, money would never be a problem again. They'd cover all my ugly parts. My drug record. My broke-ness and broken-ness. I brushed my uneasiness away.

After asking Mom to wait in the lobby, Dr. Franklin had me lie back on the operating bed and open my mouth. I stared up at the strip of bright white lights on the ceiling as he wrenched out my baby tooth with a pair of pliers, turned on what sounded like a power drill, and proceeded to slowly sand down my teeth, bone particles filling the air. When he was finished, he brought out the tray of off-white veneers his assistant had recommended and cemented them one by one over my newly flattened teeth. The whole process took about two hours. It was heaven.

Finally, he had me sit back up and placed a mirror in my hand. My heart pounded as I brought it up and pried my lips open. It took a second for what I was looking at to sink in. The veneers didn't merely close the gaps in my teeth, they also made my face fuller, my jaw rounder instead of tense and jammed tight, like I usually kept it. I scrutinized my reflection, turning from side to side. I looked like *myself*.

I looked like the real me, not that other, shame-filled version of me I'd been living as before. A startled giggle shot out of my mouth. Instinctively, I reached up to cover it with the back of my hand, but I stopped and lowered it halfway. I didn't need to hide ever again.

Dr. Franklin summoned Mom from the waiting room, and within minutes, she and half of the office were hovering over me, oohing and aahing.

"Amazing work!" they patted his back.

"It's incredible!"

"You're a genius, Doctor!"

"Precioso," Mom said, kissing my cheek. "Mi niño lindo."

A flash went off. I was back against the blank wall for my After picture with Dr. Franklin's assistant. She snatched the Polaroid from the camera and waved it in the air, then fit it into a plastic sleeve inside a binder next to dozens of other clients' Before and After photos. It reminded me of a yearbook, all our smiles vulnerable and self-conscious. As I stared at my Before photo, a strange pang of grief shot across my chest. I'd been that person my whole life. Whatever I'd felt about myself over the years, they'd kept me alive through everything.

Sitting in Mom's truck as we drove home that day, the world beyond the passenger seat window seemed to glow with possibility. Wildflowers bloomed along the edges of retention ponds, flocks of egrets swam across the tangerine sky. That week I laughed the loudest at everyone's jokes at school, savoring the new sensation of my jaw growing sore. I was the first to volunteer to work out problems on the board so my classmates could get a better view of my smile. Some offered compliments, most didn't notice a difference. I'd thought their opinions would matter to me more, but they didn't. At least, they didn't like before, when I measured my self-worth by their approval. I had $8,000 teeth now. There was no denying *my* worth.

On a sunny afternoon not long after the procedure, while I was still floating on the high of my transformation, Mom and I went to Saks Fifth Avenue to use a coupon they'd sent her in the mail. Ordinarily, I didn't even like walking through Saks to get to the other stores inside the mall. The prices intimidated me, the bored rich ladies sighing miserably as they rifled through racks of European designers. But those things also made Saks a safe space in a way. Nobody made a scene there. You had to be on your best behavior. As Mom and I stood at the Clinique counter waiting for someone to help us, a voice in the pit of my stomach told me it was time.

Do it, the voice said. *You're going to have to eventually. Come on. She's not going to freak out around all these rich white bitches. Get it over with now.*

"Mamá?" I heard myself say. "I have to tell you something."

"Yeah?" she answered while looking around for a salesclerk.

My legs started shaking, preparing to make a run for it. But the voice was right. I couldn't keep postponing the conversation forever. I laid my head on my mother's shoulder and held it there for a few more seconds, breathing in her sweet perfume, just in case she'd never let me do that again.

"I think I like boys," I told her. "I think I'm gay."

Right then a salesclerk appeared in front of us. Mom's posture stiffened. I lifted my head to try to read her face. "Okay," she said, then dug through her purse for her sunglasses and put them on, I understood, to cry. The salesclerk didn't seem to notice. Behind her sunglasses, Mom acted totally fine, cheerful even. She accepted the samples the woman offered like nothing had happened, and in the end, we left the store with a three-month supply of face wash and several bags of free makeup that came as a gift with purchase. All paid for with credit.

Afterward we walked through the mall holding hands, not speaking. I assumed she was processing what I'd said, but the fact that she hadn't pulled me to the car yet buoyed me. She didn't disown me or kick me out. Just a few tears, but maybe those were normal. Wasn't coming out supposed to be sad? The moment we entered the next store, I grabbed a random pair of jeans from a stack and fled to the dressing room. Inside, I sat with them folded on my lap, laughing. I did it, the thing I was most afraid of, and she'd said it was okay.

It wasn't, though. That night I heard her sobbing on the phone with an aunt in Nicaragua. Over the next few months, she'd begin to avoid me at home, leaving food for me in the microwave after work and disappearing into her room, locking the door behind her. My mother was born in a country where it was illegal to be gay. When she immigrated to Miami in the '80s, the queer community was in the throes of the AIDS crisis. Like my classmates, I could see her struggling to bridge the gap between then and now. In her mind, being gay would lead to a lifetime of discrimination, if I was lucky, and death by a disease or a hate crime if I was not.

Things would get worse between us before they'd get better. There'd be long, painful screaming matches, kicked-down doors. Nights when I'd fall asleep hugging my pillow tight, remembering how close we used to be. She was my best friend, my co-conspirator. When I was younger, the mere thought of her being upset with me would have destroyed me.

And yet I wasn't destroyed. In the morning, I'd wake up, take a shower, make an effort to keep going. It's a parent's job to raise their child to the best of their abilities and prepare them for the real world. Looking back, that's what she did. What Mom had been doing, since long before I'd come out, all those years she'd modeled for me how to be clever and resourceful, to never allow anyone to make you a victim. Every time she'd told me I was beautiful, even when I didn't believe that myself. She'd given me what I needed to survive. I just hadn't thought I'd have to do it without her.

From one month to the next, something shifted inside me. It was as if I'd used up my lifetime's supply of sadness in one short, aggressive period of time and now I had to find another emotion to run on. A coldness spread around my heart, not unpleasantly so, like ice on a bruise.

All right then, I decided. If all I could ever be was the Gay Kid to my classmates, then fine, I would be exactly like the bitchy gay sidekicks on TV. So what if I couldn't win over some miserable, no-taste-having-ass losers? Obviously they were just jealous I was perfect and they were what? Peaking! At seventeen! How tragic! They'd probably end up selling fridges at Sears or some shit—of course they were mad! It wasn't my fault I was gorgeous, that they simply couldn't take me. They'd made a mistake, showing me kindness when I was the new kid. I could have kept on hating myself. Ha! If it weren't for them, I might have never known I was special.

Throughout the rest of high school, I tried to pass off my silence as haughtiness, a look I thought made me seem grown. Orlando *bored* me. Oak Ridge was *embarrassing*. When I was older, I'd move to New York where people had style and sense and were really *living*.

Until then, I made friends with the kids who, like me, were also desperate for an escape. The ones who lived in the trailer parks by the airport, who filled dollar composition books with angry poetry. Queer girls. They taught me how to skip class in the bathroom, squished into the handicap stall, that no one would stop us if we walked off campus at lunch and drove to the beach, blending in with tourists. Soon I only showed up at school enough to avoid the truancy cops and maintain my 4.0 GPA—less a reflection of my intelligence than of how little our jaded, under-resourced teachers expected of us. When I did go, I sat at a desk far in the back, feigning indifference and drinking coffee out of the travel mugs Mom stole from Starbucks to give to relatives, acting as if I were sipping on an expensive latte. In case anyone mistook my being quiet as weakness and dared say something slick to me, I maintained a running catalog of insults to shoot back with: Whose gold chain left a green ring around their neck and thought no one noticed. Which jock was rumored to have a tiny dick.

In the afternoon, I rode the bus to my new job at Auntie Anne's Pretzels at the Florida Mall, treating myself to a few staples with the money I made: checkerboard Vans, Levi's 511s, clothes that radiated a casual, generational wealth, the final touch I needed to complete my Over It costume. I kept secret how I got my veneers and pretended to love working at Auntie Anne's, my smelly, baggy uniform, customers barking orders and throwing their cash onto the counter instead of placing it in my hand. I wouldn't give anyone anything to hold against me.

Making my way through the hallways at Oak Ridge, I strutted to my locker in my tightest jeans, bouncing my freshly grown-out head of curls. I was sickening, honey! *That* bitch! Happy as a moth, crashing my body over and over against a lamp. You could not tell me I wasn't going anywhere, that my future wasn't bright. I put one foot in front of the other, stuck my chin up, and smiled with all my fake teeth.

4

HOW TO BE AN INFLUENCER IN CENTRAL FLORIDA

One day in college I awoke with a sense of clarity and purpose I had never felt before.

I was twenty-one years old, living at home with my mom, and earning minimum wage working at Auntie Anne's. One of my friends was a drama major at UCF, the local public university that had offered us poor people scholarships to attend for free, and he told me about this hot lesbian classmate of his who was making thousands of dollars creating videos online, stuff like *How to Date Long Distance* and *Shit Gay People Say*.

The next morning I opened my eyes thinking, *Wait. I'm gay people. I say things.* I'd been on my high school's morning announcements crew, where I'd learned how to edit, film, and use lights. Plus, I had veneers! It was all suddenly so obvious. I had to get YouTube famous.

#1: HAVE A TALENT

Growing up in Orlando, a short drive from the bright, promising glow of Disney, you are at some point bound to run into somebody's adorable child who can sing, dance, and do splits and twirls and shit. There's a reason N*Sync and the Backstreet Boys were formed in Central Florida and why all the classic Nickelodeon shows were shot at Universal Studios. This is a place where people aren't afraid to *dream*—usually, that dream being to get famous enough to move away. For years, I fantasized my family would put me in acting classes and push me to be a showbiz kid. With my cute curls, lisp, and ethnically ambiguous skin tone, I know I could've bulldozed those other little brats easy. Instead, I wasted the best years of my childhood watching my mom do her makeup in the bathroom, so in the end I settled on becoming a beauty influencer.

It's important you understand this was not just a funny game to pass the time for me. I squirreled away money for months to buy a video camera. In my spare time, I studied the YouTube landscape like I was preparing for law school, taking note of how gay beauty influencers had less competition breaking through than straight girls, who actually needed to be talented. It seemed all I would have to do was record myself acting like a Sassy Gay BFF and fans would come flocking to me. With my fame, I would be making a political statement, Reclaiming

My Queerness and evening the playing field, an example of how with social media, women and queers can create paths toward wealth by doing the things we love that have been undervalued by the evil patriarchy. And the greatest part was I didn't even have to be hot; in fact, the more flaws I had, the better to transform myself. Really, it was a no-brainer.

Late one night, after my mom had fallen asleep, I cracked my bedroom door open and padded across the cold tile floor into the bathroom across the hall. After eleven o'clock, the only sound in the house came from the smoke detector pleading every few seconds for a replacement battery, a sharp alarm-like screech that made me feel as if I were robbing a bank as I slid open the top drawer next to the sink. I rummaged through her makeup, pulling out various lipsticks, a crusty eye shadow kit, a bottle of Maybelline foundation, and some brushes, wrapping it all in a towel in case she woke up. Back in my room, I hid the bundle under my pillow and pushed my heavy dresser up against my door, since the lock on it had been broken for years.

My room was tiny—there was barely enough room for my bed, a nightstand, and the dresser—but I'd put a lot of effort into making it cozy, decorating it like I would have if I could afford a dorm. Piles of my favorite books littered the ground. The walls were covered from floor to ceiling with faded disco records I dug out of the clearance bins at Goodwill and fashion editorials I'd ripped from the pages of *Vogue*. Wherever there was empty space, I filled it with colorful antiques and pillar candles and costume jewelry. My room was my secret hideout, a place where I could shut the door on the rest of the world and take a breath.

And yet if I was successful, what I was about to do could expose it to millions of strangers online. I cringed, seeing my sanctuary through their eyes: the hole in the wall from when I'd leaned once and it simply *caved in*, the window with its cracked glass from hurricane debris. Churning in my gut, there was also this: although I was making strides in becoming more and more comfortable with my femininity, I'd never expressed it in such a public way before.

But I was prepared for my nerves. From my backpack, I retrieved the bottle of red wine I'd purchased from 7-Eleven earlier, uncorked it, and took a long swig.

Once I was good and tipsy, I propped my video camera on a stack of books on top of my dresser, stood directly in front of it—there wasn't space for a chair—and framed myself in the viewfinder. It was too dark in the room, so I unscrewed the shade of a nearby lamp and tilted it so that the bulb pointed directly at me, like a spotlight. Then I laid all the makeup I'd borrowed out in front of me, took another swig from the bottle of wine, and hit Record.

"HI EVERYONE," I said, trying to find a balance between perky and inviting, and at the same time keeping my voice low enough that it wouldn't carry into my mom's room next door. "WELCOME TO MY CHANNEL. IT'S ME, YOUR NEW BFF EDGAR, AND TODAY I'M GOING TO BE DOING A LOOK I'VE GOTTEN TONS OF REQUESTS FOR."

It was my first video. No one had requested anything. And I

sounded like I was auditioning for the role of Pennywise the clown in the Broadway version of *It*.

But fake it till you make it, right?

I smiled wide. "GET READY TO SEE ME TRANSFORM INTO KIM KARDASHIAN!"

I picked Kim because she was a huge star who'd bring views, though I was also banking on her celebrity appeal to distract from the fact that I wasn't really sure what I was doing.

"WHAT PEOPLE DON'T KNOW ABOUT LIPSTICK"— I got to work, drawing thick lines across my cheeks and down my nose—"IS YOU CAN USE IT TO CONTOUR."

As the minutes ticked by, I couldn't tell if the sweat accumulating on my forehead was from my anxiety or from the bright lightbulb burning an inch from my face. Still, as the bottle of wine gradually emptied, I started to feel more at ease, rubbing glittery eye shadow under my brows—"A HIGHLIGHTER DUPE," I said—and applying globs of foundation over my acne. By the time the bottle was finished and I examined my reflection in the camera's viewfinder, I may not have looked like Kim K., but a warm feeling coursed through me.

At last, I threw a towel on my head, said, "HOPE YOU EN-JOYED THIS! PLEASE LIKE AND SUBSCRIBE FOR MORE CONTENT." Then I shut off the camera.

For the next couple of months, I continued making tutorials deep into the night. It very quickly dawned on me that no one was coming to my channel for actual beauty advice, so I switched gears and leaned into more novelty videos: *How to Paint Your Face with Dollar Store Makeup. How to Transform*

Yourself into a Goth/Raver Girl/Minion. I'd sneak across the hall to raid my mom's makeup drawer, then go back into my room, open a bottle of Arbor Mist, and go at it. Little by little my subscriber count rose, until eventually I had almost thirty. It wasn't much, and I hadn't made any money, but even so, it was nice to have an excuse to play around with makeup, something I wouldn't have had the courage to do on my own.

One night I was in the middle of filming a tutorial, face half-painted, when I heard my mom's bedroom door open. I froze. It was past two a.m. I could picture her standing there, gawking at the bright lights spilling out from the crack under my door, wondering what was going on.

She turned the doorknob, but the dresser blocked her from entering. "What are you doing?" she said. "Open the door."

I panicked. After coming out to her in high school, we'd finally reached a place in our relationship where the subject of my queerness didn't make the two of us want to get in our cars and drive in opposite directions. But to come out as . . . whatever *this* was—that might be too far.

I thought quick. "I'm filming a movie!" I said, while as quietly as possible I scrubbed my face with a towel and flung all her makeup into a dark corner of my closet.

"A movie?" she asked, sounding more concerned than before.

"Yeah! Mamá, I'm recording! I'm helping a friend with a school thing. I need silence."

Maybe she was too tired to argue, because all she said was, "Oh, all right," before shuffling back into her room.

After that, I quit, knowing I wouldn't be able to use the same excuse again.

#2: HOLD ON TO YOUR ETHICS

I had already spent a whole paycheck on a camera and editing software, so I decided that what I needed to do was reinvent myself, this time as a social justice influencer.

Twenty-one years of living in the South had instilled in me tons of beliefs I could mine for content. I was adamant about voting, if only to be petty because the other side made it so hard to. I thought war was bad, but slapping someone could be okay, specifically if they were a man. I didn't like guns.

My friend Elyse had been encouraging of my videos in the past, inviting me over to do face masks with her and give me makeup advice. She was only three years older, but I thought of her as a protective big sister. Elyse looked out for me, like on one of my first nights out at a bar, when I stared at the drink specials scrawled on a whiteboard, confused and a little hungry, before turning to ask her if a PBR was a type of sandwich.

"Is that like a PB&J?" I'd asked. "Cool! I didn't know they had food here. What's the R stand for? Raspberry?"

"You're so funny," Elyse said, laughing as if we were both in on a private joke, then strode up to the bartender and ordered us a round.

She was always teaching me things like that—how to make your dumb friend feel less embarrassed—which made me think she'd be a good partner to make social justice videos with.

That, and she was gorgeous. Cuban, with dark broody eyes and raven-black hair she wore pulled back to show off her widow's peak. I implicitly trusted any Caribbean woman with a resting get-out-my-face face, see: any restaurant where the takeout container is a paper plate wrapped in foil.

I don't know why Elyse agreed to partner up with me, considering she could have done it alone, but I didn't question it. Her boyfriend even volunteered to let us use his new house to film. He'd recently moved in, and his living room made for the perfect set, since at the moment there was only a small well-loved couch pushed up against a beige wall. After pitching each other ideas, Elyse and I chose to do a talk show where we'd discuss the latest social justice issues sweeping through the country and offer our perspectives. Our show would be similar to *The View,* but with two sweaty nonfamous people in somebody's empty living room in Florida.

We'd heard rumors that a new, all-female *Ghostbusters* was in production, and men on the internet were really pissed off about it for some reason, so for our first video, we prepared by smoking a bunch of weed and watching the original to see what was precious about it. Afterward, the plan was to record a recap and have a conversation about the pervasiveness of misogyny and how it's evolved over the years.

By the time we sat down to film the video, I swore I was Diane Sawyer. In my memory, we unpacked what comedy meant in the 1980s, spoke passionately about the unfair limits placed on women/queers/people of color whose stories are only valued for their trauma, and championed the artists today who were pushing through those barriers.

The next day I watched the footage, horrified. It was an hour and a half of us stoned out of our minds and speaking incoherently.

"Listen, I'm a MAN and only MEN can be *Ghostbusters*!" I cackled into Elyse's shoulder at one point, doing an impression of a comment I'd read online.

"Excuuuuse me," she responded. "*I* can bust too! Women have RIGHTS now!"

I attempted to soberly edit our high-talk down to our most articulate five minutes, but it was clear to me that our video wasn't going to make a difference in the world. More likely, we would end up on Reddit, where some pyscho would track down our address and come murder us for clout. For the first time since we became friends, I saw an opportunity to return the favor and protect Elyse like she did me. I dragged the video to my trash folder and closed my laptop.

#3: ALLOW YOURSELF TO BE VULNERABLE

I wasn't looking for another friend the night I posted a craigslist ad in the men-seeking-men personals section. I was trying to take advantage of my mom going to Miami and leaving the house to me to have loud, anonymous sex. I gave my age and location and uploaded a recent photo of myself. "Send a pic and what you're into," I wrote in the ad.

By midnight, there were a half a dozen emails in my inbox. The most recent had a bathroom mirror selfie attached. The guy in the photo wore a T-shirt with a screen print of a girl in an American flag bikini. The light from his cellphone's flash blacked out his face. Toothpaste splatters surrounded his dark reflection, like stars to his lunar eclipse.

I asked if he had a clearer pic.

Let's meet up, he replied.

Again, I requested a clearer picture.

A few minutes later he wrote back: *Why don't we meet up and go from there?*

Just one more, I told him, deciding that if he didn't send one where I could actually see what he looked like, I'd stop wasting my time and move on to the next email.

But he did. The second photo showed a man reclined on a plaid couch wearing cargo shorts and an FSU sweatshirt. His lips were tinted blue from whatever he was drinking out of the plastic Solo cup in his hand. Despite the bro-iness of it all, he was cute. I wondered why he hadn't sent this picture to begin with, then pushed the question out of my mind. I wasn't about to spend the rest of the night going back and forth, and the guys in the other emails might be duds.

When he showed up, knocking lightly on the front door, it was around one a.m. I hurried to answer in my tank top and sweatpants, eager to tear those ugly shorts off of him. In the dark, a stranger stood nudging at my welcome mat with steel-toed boots. He wasn't the guy from the picture, but with his construction worker musk and thick fire hydrant arms, it was like I'd ordered a Big Mac and gotten a MacBook. He wasn't what I asked for, but wasn't he better?

There are people out there who would have known exactly the right thing to do in this type of situation. People who had mentors growing up, people who watched true crime documentaries or were born with even the tiniest self-preservation instinct.

"Heeeey," I said, moving aside for my new boyfriend to come in. "What's your name again? Sorry, I don't remember if you told me in your email."

"No names," he said.

I nodded, both nervous and a little turned on. I led him down the narrow hallway to my room and sat down on my bed.

"So . . ." I smiled up at him.

He stayed standing and looked around with a strange expression in his eyes. I never had people over and assumed he was admiring my maximalist decor. The pages from *Vogue* on the walls. The fake fish tank plants I'd arranged along my windowsill.

"Does this place have a bathroom?" he asked absurdly.

"Um, yeah?" I answered.

He suggested we have sex in there as opposed to my bed.

"Why?" I threaded my fingers in his.

He kept looking around my room. "Because" was all he said.

"Are you sure? No one's going to bother us here." I patted the mattress with my other palm. "And these sheets are really soft. They're from Amazon."

He was unimpressed.

"Okay, whatever," I said, and made a mental note to do a better job screening craigslist dudes next time. I got up and instructed him to wait while I went to the bathroom to freshen up.

As soon as the door closed behind me, I spun around to do damage control. It hadn't occurred to me we'd end up in there. I wrapped my hands with toilet paper and wiped the sink of the hair trimmings I'd left from shaving before he arrived, then with my arm I swiped all the Precious Moments angel figurines my mom kept on display on the counter into a drawer: a problem for later. It was only while spraying air freshener that I began to register the legit danger of what was happening. This guy had lied about who he was. And he was twice my size. What if he wanted to bring me into the bathroom because it was a contained space, easier to clean the blood? I shot a friend a check-in-on-me-in-an-hour text and stashed a nail file behind the toilet, just in case. When I was finally done, I examined the area. It was . . . it was still a bathroom.

I opened the door again. "*Readyyyy,*" I cooed.

He stepped inside and the bath mat made a cartoonish squelching sound we both politely ignored. I'd forgotten to wring it. He undressed in silence, pulling down his blue jeans and stripping off his shirt to reveal a farmer's tan. I imagined him at work, a bead of sweat trailing down his hairy chest, past his soft belly down to his bulge, gathering flavor.

"You gonna get naked?" he asked.

"Right," I said, and quickly wriggled out of my sweatpants.

He grabbed my dick and cradled it in his hands approvingly as it grew harder, then without further small talk, he bent over, gripped the towel rack, and splayed his legs apart.

"All right, fuck me," he said over his shoulder. "Dámelo. I want it."

The bath mat squished under my feet as I moved over behind him. His skin was warm, covered in small, tender goosebumps. I kissed the back of his neck, his broad shoulders. I tried to turn his face to the side to kiss his lips, but he didn't budge. He kept his eyes on the white bathroom wall in front of him. "Hurry up," he said. "Just do it."

I didn't have a condom on. We hadn't done any foreplay to get him ready. Suddenly I got the feeling he hadn't done this before. *Just do it* was for Nike ads and porn, not anal sex. Everyone knew that. "Hold on. We at least have to use protection."

"Yeah, okay," he conceded. He rubbed his butt against my dick. "But hurry, I'm horny."

I spread him open, applying lube with my fingers.

"Tell me if it hurts and I'll stop," I whispered into his ear.

When I eventually penetrated him, his back tensed. He groaned and clawed at the towel rack. I tried to detach myself, but he grabbed my ass and pulled me in deeper.

"Hurry up. Come inside me. Please."

"Is this okay?" I asked after a few seconds of the gentlest thrusting I could muster.

"It's . . .," he mumbled through gritted teeth. "Keep going."

I held on to his waist, which had gone cold and slippery in my hands. I felt as if I were fucking a hard-boiled egg. Again, the possibility that he'd never done this before crossed my mind. Now it doubled back and sat there. My first time bottoming hadn't been special. In fact, it'd been with a stranger in a bathroom too. I'd always regretted it hadn't been sweeter, though lately I'd resigned myself to the difference between what queer people want and what we get. The thought unearthed a frustration I'd long ago buried inside me. This man looked over thirty.

Was this really how he wanted to lose his virginity? He deserved *more*. We all did. I wondered what I could say to him, what I would've liked for my first to have said to me.

"You're so perfect," I blurted out, then collapsed onto his back, faking an orgasm.

We dressed quickly and headed back to my room. As he wiped the sweat from his forehead, I figured I might as well ask. "Why did you want to have sex in the bathroom? Is that a fetish of yours? Not judging. Just curious."

His hands were inside his pockets. I could see him fingering his keys.

"Yeah, it is," he said.

I didn't believe him. It must have shown on my face. Maybe he figured he didn't have anything left to lose, because he bit his bottom lip and said, "Well, I didn't want you to record me." He raised a finger toward my nightstand. On top of a stack of books, my camera was pointed directly at the bed. I'd taken advantage of having the house to myself for a few days to restart my makeup tutorials. I'd made one the night before, using my bed as my seat, and hadn't put the camera away yet. But it was off. Wasn't that obvious?

What? I thought. Then immediately, *Oh.*

No.

No no no.

In an instant, the past few hours replayed in my mind.

He was closeted, that much I'd guessed. He had to have been too nervous to send me a real photo of himself, so he sent me one of someone else, someone slightly less attractive. That way when I met the actual him, I wouldn't be upset. Even now he was nervous I was secretly collecting evidence against him. I wanted to have sex on my Amazon sheets, and he thought I was going to *blackmail* him. I barely understood how to send *regular* mail.

It would've been easy to say he was being paranoid, but it's not like there weren't creeps out there. Scrolling through porn sites in the past, I'd seen videos with titles like *Hidden Cam Captures Straight Guy at Urinal* and *Locker Room Jocks Don't Realize They're Being Recorded.*

"I promise I would never do that," I assured him. "The camera's off. You can check."

His eyes surveilled my room, seemingly searching for other places where I could have stashed recording equipment. The slits of my closet door. My ceiling fan.

"Trust me," I told him.

But neither of us had a reason to trust each other. We were strangers.

He lowered his head, as if to continue concealing his identity. I walked him out and watched him climb into his car, feeling guilty. What if I'd freaked him out? What if he never felt safe to try again? I wished I hadn't bought that stupid camera. All it'd done was make mess after mess. *It's not always going to be like this!* I wanted to call out. *I swear, there are other people who aren't as awkward. Don't give up because of one idiot!*

Maybe I was blowing my influence on him out of proportion, but as he pulled out of the driveway onto the road, I decided to shut up and say nothing. The best thing I could do for him was let him forget he ever met me.

5

ALLIGATOR TEARS

We were the girls who showed up to the club ten minutes before they started charging cover, running across the parking lot to make it through the door in time. "Bitch, go!" we screamed, the frayed edges of our cropped T-shirts rolled up to our belly buttons like curled tongues. "I'm not trying to pay ten dollars!" There was Arturo, the nice Cuban boy who spent eight hours a day folding onesies at the Baby Gap. Luis, the Dominican princess, with juicy C-cup pecs that closeted dads lustily side-eyed at his job bartending at a restaurant. And the final member of our Caribbean girl group, me, the Nica-Rican mutt. I worked at the Flip Flop Shop at the Florida Mall and kept a pair of shoes in my car so the second I clocked out I could change and go.

It wasn't only about avoiding cover. I liked when the three of us got to the club early and no one was around because it was like everything there was just for us. The constellation of disco balls spinning lazily in the ceiling. The ridiculously loud house music making the sticky black floors tremble. And because gay bars in Orlando pretty much all had that same wannabe–South Beach aesthetic: the fake neon palm trees, the off-white VIP couches, the flashing strobe lights. Arturo would pull me toward the closest bartender before happy hour ended, Luis excused himself to go off to do his first putivuelta of the night even though nobody had arrived to hit on him yet.

Cut to Arturo and me giggling over whiskey sours, rehashing the latest work drama.

I'd start: *Oh my god, this gay couple came into the store this morning and got into a huge fight about what sandals to wear for their beach wedding. One of them stormed out CRYING. I wish somebody loved me like that . . .*

Then Arturo: *Today they made all the Baby Gap employees have a meeting about shoplifters. I was like, okay, what do you want me to do? Tackle somebody's abuela 'cuz she stole some socks? The fuck! If I catch someone, I'm gonna ask them to steal some for me, too!*

We'd sit there at the bar, sucking on ice cubes, our glossy eyes sweeping over whichever club we were at as it gradually filled up: Parliament House, Savoy, Southern, Pulse. Back then there was something to do every night. Manic Mondays. Wicked Wednesdays. Flesh Fridays.

But Latin night was the best, when the DJ switched out Madonna for salsa and reggaeton, the scent of Acqua di Gio assaulting you as soon as you stepped through the door. Everyone drunk on tequila sodas, shirts half-unbuttoned. That inevitable moment Thalía's "¿A Quién le Importa?" came on, and no matter where we were, the three of us rushed to the dance floor with our fists in the air to sing along. Luis grinding up against some man in Wranglers. Arturo's glasses sliding down his nose as he twirled in bliss. Beads of sweat dripping off my curly hair.

2016 always comes back to me this way:

I'll be out at a gay bar, tipsy and surrounded by smiling queer people, when out of nowhere an old, familiar ache will spread through my chest. Something will feel wrong about the picture. The room emptier than it should be. I'll look around, searching for what's missing, and suddenly I'll be twenty-four again, back in Orlando at Pulse. And it's like I'm there. Like it's any other Latin night besides the one it will never not hurt to think about. And dancing next to me is a Puerto Rican dude with the prettiest brown eyes. His customers at the salon where he performs miracles call him "the God of Hair." There's the twenty-two-year-old who runs the rides at Harry Potter World, wand tucked into his back pocket. There's a nurse; there's a drag queen; there's a mother of eleven, out with her queer son to show him he doesn't have to hide anything from her, a cool mom. There's a girl fresh out of high school who has plans to play ball in college, just a kid.

And we're dancing together. Laughing, like we've been waiting all week to let it out. Not a single one of us worried if speaking Spanish or the sight of us kissing might piss someone off. It's happened enough times by now that I know the moment will pass. Soon I'll be in the future again and the room will still be too empty. So I try to hold on to them as long as I can. Their faces. Voices. What they were like when they were happy and safe and free. I'm tired of hearing the same stories that reduce their lives to their deaths. Just for a little while, I want to remember the time before Pulse was the place where they were lost, back when we went there to be saved.

By 2016, I'd been working at the Flip Flop Shop for around a year.

The day I applied, I woke up early to wipe the nail polish off my fingers and iron a pair of khaki pants and a long-sleeve white button-up that I hadn't touched since graduating high school. At the mall, I walked past the stores where I wouldn't have stood a chance no matter what I wore—Sports Authority, Abercrombie—handing out copies of my résumé to any manager who would see me. After a few hours, I hadn't had much luck and was getting ready to go home when the smell of something sweet grabbed my attention. It was wafting out of a store I'd never heard of before. The sign at the entrance read COME IN. FREE YOUR TOES! Inside, a woman with a short-cropped afro stood behind the register staring out at the shoppers passing by, a drowsy look in her eyes. Her seashell necklace matched the vaguely tropical music playing in the shop.

"Hi there," the woman said. She seemed to wake up as I wandered into the store, stepping toward me in a pair of faded leather flip-flops. "Those are some cute shoes."

I couldn't tell if she was making fun of me for the Payless loafers I'd worn for my job hunt. They had tassels dangling from the front that I'd been hoping would fool someone into thinking I had style. "Oh, thanks," I blushed. "I wish I could wear flip-flops to work like you."

"Yeah." She curled her lips politely. "I'm really lucky."

Hundreds of flip-flops hung from racks on the walls between videos of people surfing and throwing up peace signs. I turned around and grabbed a random pair from a rack to buy myself more time in the shop, swallowing my horror as I read the number on the price tag: $112.

"These are . . . *nice,*" I said, putting them back as gently as if they were made of glass, then turned to face the woman again and scanned her name tag discreetly: Jasmine. "It smells like the beach in here." I tried to change the subject. "I think I smelled the shop from outside."

"It's the coconuts." Jasmine nodded toward a black box under the cash register. A puff of vapor shot out of the top. "We have an aromatherapy machine blowing the scent around."

"Smart," I told her, seizing that opening. "I used to work at Auntie Anne's Pretzels, and the smell of cinnamon sugar was like a people magnet." I smiled big so she could see my expensive fake teeth and tried to sound outgoing and customer-friendly, extending my hand to shake. "Are y'all hiring, by the way? I'm Edgar. I swear I don't always dress like this."

Jasmine turned out to be the manager, and after asking me a couple of questions about my retail experience (I made up a lie about working at an aunt's fashion boutique a few summers in a row and that I spoke Portuguese), she invited me to interview the next day.

A week later I was hired.

To prepare, Jasmine gave me a four-inch-thick binder to memorize, full of information about the different products that we carried, everything from materials used to brand ambassadors. Quickly I realized that though my job was to sell tourists flip-flops, when a pair could go for $200, the job was really to sell them a lifestyle. I had to convince them they weren't simply purchasing footwear, but were taking a step toward becoming whoever they wanted to be.

"These are the kind *Oprah* wears," I'd tell the stressed, sunburned moms who entered the shop, escorting them to a bench where they could rest their feet, swollen from waiting in line for hours at the theme parks. "They're memory foam. Like walking on clouds, right?"

"This brand is called Olukai because they're from Hawaii," I'd tell the dads, parroting the non-Polynesian manufacturer's story about how "they basically took the footprints people left in the sand at the beach and designed technology to make sandals. *The Rock* wears them."

Often customers saw our prices and immediately laughed out loud, rolling their eyes at me like I was the CEO and not just a twenty-four-year-old making nine dollars an hour. That's when I'd lean in conspiratorially and say, "I know. Before I worked here, I would have neverrrr paid this much. I used to wear those Old Navy ones that fall apart after a week. But this is *Florida*. We *live* in flip-flops. They're like *our sneakers*. How much do you pay for shoes?"

Throughout our shifts, the store was monitored by the franchise owner, a white lady named Stacy who watched employees through security cameras and emailed us orders like a weird, boring version of *The Sims*. "Let's push more sunblock, gang! Goal today is twenty-six hundred dollars!!" she'd write. Or "Seeing a lot of talking. Has inventory been done yet?" Inventory consisted of counting every pair of flip-flops in the store by hand, a required daily task to ensure that nothing had been stolen, either by customers or us. There were thousands. It was tedious, but still, I found a strange pride in knowing something about every make and model.

Take Havaianas: simple, classic flip-flops with cute colors and patterns. Our most "economical," the word I preferred to use when someone asked for something "cheap."

Or Reefs: another classic. A step up from Havaianas, because the strips between the toes on these were fabric, so they didn't chafe.

Fit Flops: pricier, but an investment in the future. They were designed by podiatrists. Great for plantar fasciitis and heel spurs. The look of relief on a customer's face when they tried a pair for the first time made me feel a little less small as I got on my knees to help put them on.

I could continue, but I'll spare you. The point is that any job, even at the Flip Flop Shop, requires a level of skill. Someone has to know these things. Someone has to be there when your kids won't stop crying and your feet hurt and no one else cares about your pain.

Because the shop was tiny, I worked alone on weekdays starting at nine a.m., tagging out with another co-worker at midafternoon. By then, since there was no employee bathroom in the shop, my bladder was close to bursting, and I'd run to the nearest one by the Apple Store. Once when I couldn't hold it, I peed myself and had to tie a hoodie around my waist.

Most of my co-workers were college age, all but one of us a person of color. There were times when I was grateful for that. Having some shared experiences allowed us to form fast bonds, and at least we had each other to talk to about the casual racism from customers, the "A week in Florida and I'm almost as tan as you!"s and the "Okay, but where are you *really* from?"s. Other times, I'd be strolling through the mall and couldn't help noticing all the Black and brown locals serving white tourists. In the food court, at kiosks, mopping. The same drowsy, worn-out look as Jasmine that I came to have, too, their own Stacys watching through cameras, reminding them that "if there's time to lean, there's time to clean." Then a smothering feeling would overtake me, as if some horrible, ancient force had wrapped its arms tight around me and everyone I loved and wouldn't let go, and it'd take all of me not to say *fuck this* and leave.

In those moments when life seemed to close in from all sides, I would walk with my head down to the food court Starbucks, avoiding eye contact with anyone around me. I would hand over my credit card and purchase a six-dollar coffee, trying not to think about my mom waking up at three a.m. to make six-dollar coffees at the airport, or about the fact that no matter how many thousands of dollars of flip-flops I sold or emails Stacy sent saying she was proud of us, I still couldn't afford a car with functional AC. I would carry my drink to the upstairs dining area, take a seat at a table, and focus on how nice it was to be able to treat myself every once in a while. I would breathe in and out and enjoy my little bit of capitalism. And after some time, a sense of calm would wash over me, and the world would sort of go quiet.

I can't remember exactly how we met, but in my dream origin story, Luis, Arturo, and I were once babies asleep in cribs all over Orlando, cocooned inside blankets, preparing to emerge. Then one day we woke up, blinked in delight at our transformed bodies, our clothes bursting at the seams, and fluttered out into the street, wide-eyed and horny like newborn butterflies.

But I mean, it was probably at a gay bar.

That year, we started most nights at Luis's. He lived on the outskirts of downtown, in a three-bedroom rental house that might have been decent before his rotating cast of crust punk roommates slowly trashed it. Crushed Miller Lite cans littered the ground, all their furniture was coated with a grimy layer of cigarette soot and dust. The first time Luis invited Arturo and me over and I saw the yellowed mattress on the living room floor where he slept, I should've been grossed out. Instead, my insides lit up with jealousy. It looked like perfect freedom to me.

Arturo and I lived with our moms, and though it was normal for children to stay home until they were married in the countries our parents emigrated from, that was how straight people did things. They didn't have anything to hide, whereas I felt awkward being gay around my mother, regardless of her efforts to show me she accepted me by playing *The Ellen Show* loudly on TV. I could tell she was still slightly uncomfortable with the person I was becoming—the eyebrows I'd tweezed until they were blade thin, my ever-shrinking outfits—and while I was in the process of shedding my own discomfort with my queerness, even the suspicion that she wished I was different stung. I wanted to be able to invite guys over without fearing what she'd think, to walk around in booty shorts and a crop top belting Ariana Grande lyrics, like Luis did.

Maybe he sensed how desperate I was, because he didn't act annoyed by how often I came over, practically spending as much time at his place as mine. In return, Arturo and I tried to make ourselves useful, helping Luis shave the parts of his back he couldn't reach and driving him to the Belle Isle Bayou, the Cajun restaurant by the airport where he bartended. We took care of each other: with a ride, a meal, a place where we could let our guards down.

One night the three of us were sitting on lawn chairs in Luis's front porch, painting our nails, scrolling through Grindr on our phones. The bare lightbulb above us flickered in and out.

"Be honest." I ruffled my hair and crossed my legs, then uncrossed them, trying to appear nonchalant. "Am I ugly? Would y'all date me if you didn't know me?"

"Babe, stop," Luis said, blowing on his wet nails. "You are such a cutie! With your little curls. Who wouldn't wanna gobble you up?"

"Then how come nobody I message writes me back?" I leaned in to show them my Grindr profile. *Vers bottom. Double Pisces. Looking for the love of my life, or NSA fun.*

"It's because you don't have pictures," Arturo said after one quick glance through his giant abuelita-style gold-rimmed glasses.

"Yeah," Luis agreed. "No one responds to blank profiles, duh." He showed me his own profile pic: wearing a teeny Speedo at the beach, his pecs pushed together like porn star breasts. One word: *Hosting*. His phone buzzed with incoming messages: *Where?? Free now???? Into???*

"I can't have a picture," I sighed.

I'd recently started substitute teaching to make a little extra money on my days off from the shop, maybe save enough to one day have my own mattress on the floor. The paranoid person in me worried what would happen if one of my older students found out about my Grindr and spread my profile around as a prank or, equally mortifying, went to the mall and saw me, the adult paid to babysit them at school, behind the register wearing a name tag. I could already imagine their jokes. *Mr., didn't I see you the other day? What's that store where you work called? The* Flop *Shop, right? 'Cause you're such a flop! Ha-ha.*

"It's cool." I slid my phone into my pocket. "I'm saving myself for marriage anyway."

"Oh how precious," Luis sang in an exaggerated Long Island accent, clutching his neck as if there were pearls there. "My daughter, getting married!"

"What are y'all trying to do tonight?" said Arturo. "I'm not tired. I can take us somewhere," he offered.

We cycled through ideas. None of us were hungry. It was a weeknight, so the bars were probably dead. "We could go to Club O," I suggested. Club Orlando was a twenty-four-hour gay bathhouse with a sauna and huge pool. The entrance fee was like twenty-five dollars, though.

"If you wanna go swimming," Luis said, "I know a good spot."

"Where?" I asked.

"Super close." Luis grinned. "Trust me, it's cute."

Minutes later we were piled into Arturo's car, driving through downtown Orlando, Luis guiding him from the passenger seat. Behind them, I quietly opened Grindr one more time to see if I'd gotten any replies to the dozens of messages I'd sent, then closed it quickly again and turned to the window, embarrassed. Soon the businesses along the side of the road gave way to long patches of dense forest. We were headed away from the city, toward the outer suburbs.

"This is it, turn here," Luis said after a while. I followed his eyes to the entrance sign outside a sleepy-looking apartment complex. It had one of those fake fancy names that all the raggedy affordable housing projects I grew up in had: something like the Shepherd's Inn or Oasis Estates. But this place might not have been pretending. I couldn't see any Puerto Rican flags anywhere. No cars with missing hubcaps or kids crying on swings. It was cute or whatever.

Arturo drove past the leasing office and parked in an empty spot far back by the community pool. There were a few residential units a short walk away, but otherwise, the place was secluded. Luis grabbed the six-pack of beers we brought with us and got out, smiling triumphantly. The three of us headed toward the pool, stopping when we reached the security gate.

Beyond it, the lights were off, but the water's silver-blue surface glowed under the moon.

Arturo wrapped his fingers around the gate's white bars and shook them. "Ay, what do we do?" He turned to Luis. "Do you have a key?"

"I don't live here girl," Luis said. He handed Arturo the six-pack, shoved his foot between a set of bars, jumped over, then ran around to open the door for us.

Arturo and I gave each other a look.

We tiptoed behind him, careful to keep our giggles low as we peeled off our shirts and abandoned them on some empty suntanning chairs. I wanted to seem chill and carefree, but my heart raced in my chest, imagining one of the bougie residents spotting us and calling the cops. I hated how in my head I got, always envisioning the worst possible outcomes.

I chugged a beer in one long gulp, trying to ease my anxiety, and walked over to the edge of the pool in the swim trunks Luis had let me borrow, dipping my toes inside. The water was warm. The pool must have been heated. On the other side of the gate, cicadas buzzed in the trees scattered throughout the parking lot, their noisy rattles like a thousand people whispering.

Psst psst psst psssstt . . .

I peered back at Arturo and Luis, who were finishing undressing by the tanning chairs. "If someone calls the cops, I'm running!" I shouted. "I don't know y'all!"

"Yes you do!" Arturo shouted back. "You know us, EDGAR RUBEN GOMEZ! I'm gonna tell them your address and Social Security number. We're going down together, bitch!"

"Fine, I'm going home," I said. I waved goodbye to them and took a step forward, plunging into the pool. As my body sank to the bottom, I tucked my knees into my stomach, holding on to myself as tight as I could, my heartbeat slowing to a steady rhythm inside the water's dark, cozy silence. For a while, I stayed tucked into myself like that. Trying not to think. To not do anything but ration out the remaining air in my lungs. Stay alive, one burning second at a time.

Suddenly, somewhere far away, I heard a muted splash, and another. I let go of my knees and kicked back up to the top of the pool, breaking through the water's surface into the humid Florida night. Ripples spread around the spots where Arturo and Luis had jumped in. I brushed the limp wet hair from my eyes and waited. Luis rose up first, spitting out water through the gap in his two front teeth like a fountain, then Arturo, looking naked without his glasses.

"This sucks!" Arturo laughed, squinting around blindly. "I hate this!"

We took turns diving. Fetching beers. Fighting mosquitoes.

Luis doggy-paddled to the edge of the pool, pulled himself out, and ran to the chairs, then dug through our pile of clothes until he found his phone. He ran back to the pool, his lips spreading into a playful smirk, and stuffed the phone into a sneaker with the camera facing us.

"Hurry up. Get ready!" he squealed as he adjusted the sneaker.

Arturo and I swam to the deep end, where a steel ladder descended eight feet into the pitch-black pool floor, and positioned ourselves on either side. "Ready!" we cooed.

"Ten seconds," Luis announced. He pressed the self-timer button on the phone's camera and ran to meet us at the ladder, stuffing himself between us.

We each struck a pose. Flash. Our eyes red dots, tongues hanging out. Someone got out of the pool to press the button again. Charlie's Angels this time, back-to-back, blowing smoke out of our pretend guns. Another flash.

"One more?" Luis winked at me. "For your Grindr?"

"Wow, sooo funny!" I splashed him with water. Still, I climbed out to set the timer. When I returned, I stayed above ground, pulled my shorts down, and slapped my ass.

Flash. Looking like drunk, messy bitches.

We would stay there for another hour, until the sound of a passing police siren made us panic, and we scrambled out of the pool, the three of us running for our clothes screaming.

I have this memory seared into my brain. It's from when I was twelve, back when I started working with my brother at the flea market after Mom's stroke. Saturdays and Sundays.

At first, we sold things we found around the house she wouldn't miss: clothes Hector and I outgrew, ugly novelty coffee mugs she'd brought home from Starbucks to give away as gifts, junk like that. But at one point, Hector figured out how to burn CDs on the computer, and so we started selling bootlegs too. Sean Paul records, P. Diddy's greatest hits, Lo Mejor de Maná. After school, I helped him by drawing covers and writing out the list of songs on sheets of paper we cut into squares and slid into the plastic sleeves we got in packs of ten at Best Buy.

One Sunday morning we brought a hundred CDs to the flea market in a crate to sell for a dollar each. It'd taken me a week to draw all the covers—our biggest batch yet. As we were setting up our fold-out table, another vendor walking by stopped and picked up a CD, examining it. I had the neatest handwriting in the eighth grade, plus I used a ruler, so I knew he was impressed. Hector went up to talk to him, and just like that, the man offered to buy all our supply, either because he felt bad for us or because he thought he could sell them for more.

Whatever the man's reason, my brother and I split the ten wrinkly ten-dollar bills he handed over to us, cackling like evil geniuses. "Stupid ass!" Hector said. The bootlegs were good but not *that* good. It was more money than we'd ever made in a sale. With that much, we could've gone home, but it was early and we still had other stuff left over, so we decided to stay.

We'd set up our table that day in a far corner of the flea market, with the Mexicans and Jamaicans. I liked it better than the scary redneck side with all the old guns and knives. Behind us, a chain-link fence separated the flea market from a small retention pond about a hundred feet away, where the runoff water from the nearby roads drained when it rained.

For the first hour, as families slowly began to arrive in their church clothes, I sat on a lawn chair next to our table wondering how to spend my cut. We still needed to put gas in Mom's truck and pay the fifteen-dollar vendor fee. After subtracting the cost of the CDs, that left me with around twenty bucks. A fortune. While Hector spoke to a customer, I got up and went to explore other tables, picking up expired perfumes and dusty

Nintendo 64 games, until eventually I found myself at the booth directly across from ours.

It was the pet guy's booth. From my seat, it had looked fun, all bright primary colors and parakeets chirping from their shiny cages. Up close, however, there was something off. A heavy, rotten stench hung from the parakeets' scrawny bodies. They banged their beaks against the metal bars, their feather coats riddled with bald spots. The pet guy—a man with a sleeve of naked lady tattoos and saggy pants covered in stains—moved around the booth, showing customers his assortment of snakes, chickens, iguanas, each one in a bleaker state than the last.

But the baby turtles were the saddest. The pet guy kept them in a fish tank full of murky brown water with a green plastic island floating inside, a little fake palm tree stuck to the middle. There were a dozen baby turtles piled on top of the island, crawling all over each other, tumbling backward as they attempted to climb up the tank's slimy glass walls. Another dozen or so fought for space in the dark water around the island. When one of the turtles raised its head to me, eyes slick with tears, my mind went blank. Without thinking, I gave the pet guy two ten-dollar bills.

I brought my baby back to the lawn chair cradled in the palm of my hand. He smelled like garbage, his shell was coated in a gross, gloopy gunk. I knew I'd love him forever. I put him down on my knee, tickling his shell with my fingertip as he chomped chomped chomped the air.

After some time, Hector came over to check on me. On instinct, I placed my hand on top of my baby to keep my secret safe, panic shooting up my spine. I hadn't thought about it until then, but my baby *was* a secret. Mom was going to be so mad at me if I brought him home. She hadn't been able to work in months. This was not how I should have spent my money.

But I couldn't give my baby back. I felt his tiny body crawling playfully under my palm. He needed me. He would be miserable at the pet booth with all the other sad turtles.

"Don't worry, you're safe," I whispered to my baby as soon as Hector left.

I looked around, trying to figure out what to do with him. When I saw the retention pond in the distance, I had an idea. I got up calmly and carried my baby hidden under my shirt. It hadn't rained in days, so the retention pond was half-empty, but as I walked toward the chain-link fence, I could see that along the edges of the water were shrubs he could make a house in, birds who could be his friends. I put my baby through a hole in the rusty wires, gently setting him on the ground on the other side. The grass barely folded beneath his weight.

"Go there." I pointed to the pond. It wasn't far. He could make it.

My baby lifted his big eyes at me, confused.

"You're free now," I said, nudging him in the direction of the water. "Go."

Then I ran back to the chair and crossed my arms and huffed. I didn't dare look back, instead focusing my attention on the customers passing by on the skinny dirt path in front of me as they moved from booth to booth. Old ladies pulling metal carts full of groceries, teenagers brooding a foot behind their parents. He was probably already at the pond, I told myself, starting his new life. I couldn't save them all, but I'd saved his. That was something.

I was still sitting there a half hour later, wishing that we'd gotten to spend more time together, when I saw a green shell inching across the dirt path. I recognized him immediately. My baby. My dumb, beautiful baby. He'd come back! He must have turned around right after I'd left him, and now he was lost, inching across the dirt path with all those people's feet threatening to trample his little body. What the hell was he doing? He was supposed to be safe. I shot out of my seat, my eyes darting from him to the sneakers crashing down around him.

Right as I was about to take a step forward, a hand descended from above and scooped him up. I followed the stained pants to a tattooed arm, up to the pet guy's scrunched-up face. He looked at my baby in his hands like *How'd you get here?* then held him up at the families walking by, waiting to see if one of them claimed him. As he searched, his eyes grazed mine.

I stood there, frozen, not sure whether I should say something. If I took him back, I could try pushing him through the fence again, but the more I thought about it, the more dangerous that plan sounded. He could get lost again. It was hot out, he had to be thirsty, his shell baking in the heat. What if there were gators in the water? One of my teachers said they were in every fresh body of water in Florida. What if he wasn't safe there either? And I still couldn't take him home.

My baby wriggled in the pet guy's hands, kicking his feet in the air. After a while, the pet guy shrugged, walked over to his booth, and deposited him back into the fish tank. My baby tucked his legs and head inside his shell as he sank to the bottom like a rock. *It's going to be okay,* I tried telling him with my mind. *Just hold on. Rich people are going to come buy you.* But he didn't move, and none of the families walking by seemed to be interested in turtles. I watched him poke his head out, look up at his siblings thrashing above him, then retreat into his shell again, regretting having set him free. Maybe it hadn't been so bad before, when all he knew was the water and the island and the fake tree. But now he'd know everything he was missing.

"Who you going to be tonight?" Arturo asked, his voice straining over the muffled sound of Daddy Yankee blasting outside the bathroom door. We were at Pulse. He hopped onto the sink counter, facing me with his Forever 21 boots swinging back and forth like an eager kid. On the wall next to him, a safe-sex poster warned, A SMILE ISN'T THE ONLY THING THAT'S INFECTIOUS.

"Who are you going to be?" was one of our favorite games to play at the club. Orlando with its never-ending stream of out-of-town visitors provided us ample people to play it with. In the past, we'd told men we were corporate attorneys from Manhattan, luxury real estate agents from L.A., *National Geographic* photographers on assignment in Florida to take photos of the dying orange trees. The fun for me wasn't in the lying, but in whether I could actually convince someone that the person standing in front of them was worth talking to. It was almost funny, seeing the shift in their eyes when they went from thinking I was no one, to surprise, to envy.

"I don't know if I want to play tonight," I told Arturo as I examined my reflection in the mirror, adjusting my curls to cover the zits on my forehead. I'd come straight from work, and my face was tired of smiling, my T-shirt stuck to my armpits with eight hours of sweat. "I feel like shit." I lowered my nose to my armpit and cringed. "Ugh, sorry, I *smell* like shit too." I squeezed a dollop of soap out of the dispenser and patted it under my arms, keeping an eye on the door.

Arturo frowned. "So . . .," he started to say, then stopped and bit his lip, as if carefully choosing his phrasing. "Luis and I have been talking."

"Yeah?"

"About you."

"Oh." I turned to face him.

"Yeah. This is awkward, and baby girl we love you, but you have to stop saying you're a piece of shit, that you suck. We, like, don't like that."

"Whaaaat?" I asked, laughing uncomfortably. "I don't do that! Do I do that?"

"I mean . . . yeah. You kind of do it a lot."

"Um, all right." I bent over to wash my hands.

"Don't be mad." Arturo hopped off the counter. "It's just . . . you're not a piece of shit, okay! And it makes us sad, because we love you and want you to know how amazing you are."

My stomach clenched. *Nope.* I went into the nearest stall, locking the door behind me.

He yelled over the divider. "You are the sweetest, smartest person I know!"

"I'm peeing!" I called out, then dropped my eyes to the floor, all of a sudden feeling exposed. Where the hell was this coming from? So what if I said I was shit? Isn't that how people talked?

Wasn't that better than burdening everybody with my feelings? Who cared that it took hours to drag myself out of bed most mornings? Or that sometimes I felt like an animatronic on the "It's a Small World" ride at Disney, like I only came to life when tourists passing by needed me to help them pick out flip-flops? I was fine. I could handle managing my insecurities in my own harmless, exciting ways: catfishing dudes on vacation, disassociating at Starbucks.

"Well you're going to hear this!" Arturo yelled through the door. "You are my best friend and perfect and I will throw you on the floor and fight you until you accept my love, bitch!"

I flushed the toilet with my foot so he wouldn't know I'd just been standing there and came out again. "Oh my god! I love you too! Damn! We don't have to be corny about it!"

Arturo wrapped his arms around me, squeezing me tight. "Yes, we do. We have to be corny." I tried wriggling free, but he squeezed tighter.

"Listen," he said. "I love you. You're amazing. I love you."

"Okay," I surrendered, leaning my head on his shoulder. I could feel his heart beating against mine under our clothes. It was nice. I wouldn't have admitted it then, but it was.

He held me a few more seconds, rubbing my back while I stared sideways at the scuffed wall behind him. Something told me we weren't the first to have a heart-to-heart where we stood, that the walls had seen boys sobbing after running into their asshole exes, girls bent over the toilet, a kind stranger holding their hair up, gently encouraging them to *Let it out. Let it out.*

I peeled my head off Arturo. "You win. I'm amazing. Happy?"

"Whatever. Just, like, believe me."

"I do." I promised myself I would at least try to.

"Cool," he said. "Let's go be gay then. I think I saw Luis at the bar talking to this man who looks like my tío."

That night ended like so many others. We drank too many neon-colored cocktails, made out on the dance floor with guys whose names we wouldn't remember the next morning. Maybe one of us said it was our birthday to see what we'd get for free. Maybe we caught one of the local queens doing a number—Roxxxy Andrews or Mr. Ms. Adrien or Lisa Lane.

At Pulse, you could be anyone. A Puerto Rican makeup artist who transformed into a glamorous Amazonian on stage. A butch lesbian, finally in a good place after some rough years. A Brazilian restaurateur with a Portuguese accent that didn't fool anyone, visiting Orlando to scout out new locations. You could be yourself, whoever you couldn't be anywhere else.

When the call came, I was sleeping.

I groaned, patting the pillow beside me until I found my phone. I was supposed to wake up in a few hours to go open the shop—that was why I'd stayed home on a Saturday, instead of closing down the bars like usual. I squinted through the dark as Arturo's name flashed on-screen beneath the time and date. June 12. Three-thirty a.m. My phone's wallpaper: the photo of him, Luis, and me blowing air-kisses from inside the pool.

A couple months earlier, Luis had moved to New York, where he was bartending and modeling, once again leading the way, daring me to imagine what was possible for us. My girl had even bought himself a bed. Only Arturo and I were left now.

I answered the call reluctantly and hung up a few minutes later, Arturo's panicked voice echoing in my ears.

He'd said to turn on the news. That there was a man. With a gun. And he'd been at Pulse, shooting people. There were police outside the club right now. He said one of our friends' moms was on TV being interviewed, asking if anyone knew where her son was. "But you weren't there," Arturo kept repeating. "I wasn't sure if . . . but . . . thank God, you weren't there."

"No," I told him, and he must have understood that I wasn't responding to what he'd said but was begging for him to stop, because he told me he'd check in on me in the morning. I set my phone down, a numbness spreading through my body, like a rush of adrenaline after an accident. I must have been in shock, or else I would've driven over to him right then. Instead I grabbed a pillow, pulled it toward my chest, and forced myself to go back to sleep—I suppose I believed that if I did that, there was still a chance that it was all a bad dream.

When I woke up, there were dozens of missed calls and texts on my phone. One was from Jasmine at the shop telling me she would cover my shift, that I could take the day off. *Thank you,* I wrote back, then I stared at the ceiling for a long time.

Arturo picked me up around noon and we drove twenty minutes away to Parliament House, one of the oldest gay bars in Orlando. We went there because we thought it would be open. It'd been a vacation resort in the '60s, before Disney built its own hotels closer to the parks and the gays took Parliament over, converted the property into a massive nightclub. They kept the on-site motel rooms and added several dance floors and a theater for drag shows. Visitors stayed at the motel overnight, so the place could never really close. When we arrived, hundreds of people were already there. Cops flanked both sides of the front door, patting folks down as they entered. I'd never seen anything like that before at Parliament. I threaded my fingers through Arturo's as we waited in line, the two of us probably thinking the same thing: *They're checking for weapons. They're worried there might be another shooter among us.*

"Do you want to leave?" I asked him.

Arturo looked back to the parking lot where we'd come from, and then at me. "Where would we go?" he said.

The club itself wasn't open, so we went straight to the outdoor courtyard, where the motel was. It was almost one by then, but guests were just waking up and coming out of their rooms. I saw a man wandering around, his eyebrows furrowed in confusion. He looked so out of place, wearing a kilt and a leather harness as he stared at the shell-shocked crowd gathered around him. It was obvious no one had told him what had happened yet. That he'd fallen asleep in last night's outfit, heard a bunch of people outside, and left his room to see what was going on. I clung to the ridiculousness of that, like it was proof that what the news was reporting was too absurd to possibly be true. Someone would have told him. This had to be a weird, elaborate prank. Our Pulse? On Latin night? No.

Arturo pulled me to one of the smaller outdoor bars to buy drinks—I couldn't believe that either, that bartenders had been called in to work on this day. At the same time, we felt obligated to support the club for giving us a place to be, and I needed something to calm my nerves. A group of friends behind us were talking about how they'd gone to try to donate blood to the victims but were turned away because gay people weren't allowed to donate blood, not even to help other dying gay people, because it was government policy to assume we all had AIDS. We tipped triple the price of our drinks and walked away, our cups already half-empty. No.

An hour later they opened the doors to the club, and the crowd in the courtyard rushed inside. The lights were off on the dance floor. There was no music playing. Above us, the disco balls in the ceiling were frozen midspin, as if time had stopped the moment the first shot was fired. The muffled sobs of the hundreds of gay people around me filled my ears. When I closed my eyes, I saw images of spilled drinks, shattered glasses, people running, red everywhere.

The list of victims hadn't been released—no one knew there were forty-nine queer, predominantly Latinx people dead yet. Some of our friends had checked in safe on Facebook, but there were others we still hadn't heard from. I felt dizzy. A frantic energy stirred inside me. Why hadn't they checked in? What if there was a second shooter here, hiding? Our blood useless. An assault rifle. Our friend's mom, asking if anyone had seen him. No no no no no.

Out of nowhere, someone whose face I couldn't see in the darkness climbed into the DJ booth. I tugged Arturo's arm. "Who is that?" I asked. "What are they doing?"

Before he could answer, the opening chords of "True Colors" by Cyndi Lauper started to play on the speakers. Arturo gasped, and I guess that's when I knew it was real, when I couldn't deny it anymore. A single tear snailed down my cheek, followed by another and another. Fat, sloppy tears fell from my eyes, over my lips, into my mouth. I cried and cried and cried. My chest heaving, all the tears I'd been carrying inside of me pouring out. I cried, thinking of all the people who'd gone to Pulse to have a break, to take the night off, and how some man . . . some man had killed them. I cried because somehow I'd underestimated how much the world hated us. I cried because a part of me knew that nothing would ever be the same again, because it wasn't fair, because I was so angry I wanted to bite someone, because I was cold, because deep down, a part of me had felt cold for years. I cried, imagining how they would have probably laughed if they knew we were all at Parliament House crying to "True fucking Colors."

And then I looked at Arturo beside me, and another tear fell from my eyes, because I could have been there alone.

"I love you," I said, hugging him.

All around us, everyone had their arms locked around each other as the song slowly faded out.

Afterward, all that was left was the sound of hundreds of us crying together on the dance floor, saying, *I love you. I love you. Te quiero. I love you so much. I know.*

By nightfall, Arturo and I were blackout drunk, stumbling along the sidewalks outside Parliament. We'd gone to the gas station a couple blocks away to get food, I think, or fresh air, and were lost, trying to get back to the club. A drag queen had told us there was going to be a show at ten o'clock, like every Sunday. There was something reassuring about that, about the fact that the show was still going to go on. I don't remember any of this. I only know because as we were walking, a reporter from NPR appeared on the sidewalk holding a microphone.

Every now and then, I revisit the interview we apparently gave to him. I picture us standing there, holding each other up. In the grainy recording on the NPR website, Arturo shares with the reporter a piece of wisdom that same drag queen had given us earlier in the day:

> She said happiness is the ultimate rebellion. And I think that the man who hurt so many of our friends last night, his goal was to make us too scared to leave our houses and to make us feel like we were alone and like our community didn't exist. And just by being here, we're proving that that's wrong.

It feels strange listening to his voice a decade later, now that Pulse is a museum and Parliament House an empty lot. Stranger that if it weren't for that recording, my memory of that night would end with us crying, and I wouldn't know there was hope, even then. That's the story I keep telling myself, because I'm afraid if I don't, I'll forget. There was a time when we were scared, the two of us stumbling down the sidewalk at night. But we weren't alone. There were always people waiting. All we had to do was let the lights in the distance remind us the way.

6

MY BODY OF WORK

The first time was in high school.

I was a junior. Sixteen or seventeen. These boys from school were throwing a house party on New Year's over winter break. I remember sitting with a girl in Spanish class one afternoon, letting her copy my worksheet, when a pair of Air Forces kicked the back of her chair. She flipped her crunchy, wet-gel curls over her shoulder and spun around.

"Oh my god, stooooop! You are sooo annoying."

"I'mma see you there, right?" one of the boys planning the party asked, throwing his hands up, all smiley and cute, before fixing his eyes on me, like *Bitch, what you staring at?*

Obviously I didn't get invited, but my friend Mikey did. He was in every club, front row at all the football games, cussing out the other schools so thoroughly even our teachers had to clap their hands to their mouths to hide their laughter. No one knew he was gay but me; he sent me a drunk text one night; girl, I felt a little bad for him. I don't really think he was drunk. But I guess that's why he offered to take me to the party. I'd kept his secret. I promised it wasn't a big deal. He said the same about the party. It was just going to be some dumb kids acting drunk on Smirnoff's. I didn't care. I wanted to see how dumb they were for myself. I wanted to be seen by anyone who didn't want me there so the next time one of them smirked and asked me what it felt like to have a dick up my ass, I could shrug and say, "Whatever, y'all are boring anyway."

The night of the party, I bit my nails down to stubs trying to figure out what to wear. All my clothes were too basic. Blue jeans. T-shirts. I settled on a black-and-white-checkered hoodie I'd gotten on sale at Goodwill even though I had no business owning it in Florida. Not basic—subtle, vintage. Just in case, I stole a few spritzes of my mom's favorite perfume, Escape by Calvin Klein. She bought herself a bottle for Christmas every year. It was the last step in her routine after she put on her uniform and did her makeup before going to work. It caught her customers at Starbucks by surprise. They didn't expect a barista to smell that good. I smiled, spraying it on my neck and wrists and chest. I was going to surprise everybody too.

Mikey picked me up an hour late, the front window of his busted-ass Toyota Corolla covered in bird shit, the backseat littered with his younger brother's toys. On the drive to the party,

I played it cool, not once mentioning where we were going, as if it didn't matter.

When we finally arrived, he found a dark spot to park on the side of the street under some trees. It was so far away we couldn't see the house, just other kids from school walking to it from their cars. Maybe it was then that it hit him what going inside with me would mean, or maybe he wasn't lying when he checked the time on his phone and said it wasn't worth it, the cops would break it up soon. Either way I was pissed. It was too risky for us to be seen together, fine, I wasn't naïve, but why did he drag me all the way there? Why did he let me get excited?

"So, um, do you wanna go anywhere else?" Mikey asked.

My stupid perfume stank up the air between us.

Fuck you, I nearly said.

But he was my ride, and I couldn't have him drop me off at home too early. I'd begged my mom to let me stay out late. If I got back after twenty minutes, she'd probably assume some shit happened, blow it out of proportion, and never let me go out anywhere again. So I gave Mikey directions to this quiet swamp close to my house where we could park on the grass and wait a while. It wasn't even midnight yet. Fireworks bloomed in the sky, illuminating the bloated Hot Cheeto bags floating on the swamp's surface.

I sat there fuming, thinking about the hours I'd spent consoling him after he came out to me. Did he forget? Because actually I lied. It *was* a big deal to be gay, and he'd find out soon how quickly everyone could change on him. I opened my mouth to tell him that, that I wasn't some doll he could pick up and play with whenever he felt like, but he must've taken it

EDGAR GOMEZ

some other way because he unbuckled his seatbelt and leaped over the coin tray to kiss me. His tongue rough, gross.

I pushed him off and scooted to the farthest edge of the seat, watching him with my shoulders pressed up against the window. He stared back at me. At my lips, the way boys do.

Then I understood. The party: a pretense. This night was always going to end like this.

I was a fiercely guarded teenager, easily riled and ready to defend myself at all times. At home, I'd filled the living room TV's DVR with rom-coms and movies about sex workers—my favorites were often a little of both: *Pretty Woman. Closer. Breakfast at Tiffany's.* I liked the predictability, how rich dudes invariably showed up to offer the women the love and security they'd been craving for so long. I especially appreciated the boldness of the sex workers. They didn't sit around waiting for their rich dudes to come. They put on their sluttiest outfits and went out looking for them. In a flash, I saw an opportunity to get even with Mikey.

I grabbed my bulge. "How much would you pay for me?" I asked.

"I—" His eyes darted around the inside of his car. "I'm sorry, what?"

I couldn't stop. It felt good to see him squirm. Taking control.

"You heard me," I said.

"Are you serious?"

I nodded, like I'd done this a thousand times before.

He coughed and examined his fingernails for a second, then pulled out his wallet, thumbed through it, and looked up at me. "I—I have twenty dollars," he said.

"That's it?" I asked. I'd been bluffing, but now that he'd agreed, I supposed twenty dollars didn't sound so bad. It was twenty dollars more than I had. "All right," I said.

I opened my door and stepped outside. Mikey scrambled out too, his clumsy feet sinking into the soft wet grass as he made his way to me. Once we were face-to-face, he dropped to his knees. Only then did it occur to me we hadn't discussed what the twenty dollars was for.

I tried to hide my shock as he unzipped my jeans and shoved my dick into his mouth, realizing he was paying to give *me* head. Right away he began to slap himself with it, gagging and moaning and looking up at me hungry for approval like we were on a porn set. Seeing him so eager to please disarmed me. Gave me secondhand embarrassment. Maybe I was embarrassed for us both. *This is it, then,* I thought. *New Year's at a swamp.* I swatted mosquitoes away and moaned politely in return, which only had the effect of encouraging him.

When enough time seemed to have passed, I said thank you and slid my briefs up without coming. The short drive back to my house was weirdly pleasant. We listened to Madonna.

▲

At the time, I worked at Auntie Anne's Pretzels at the Florida Mall. Our menu had seven types of pretzels, plus a bunch of other delicious, heart-clogging, butter-soaked treats. Everything we made had a fifteen-minute expiration date because after fifteen minutes the butter congealed, and no one was going to pay five dollars for a piece of rock-hard bread. We had to throw what we didn't sell by then into the trash, so there were always replacements to take out of the oven. During rushes, I ran back and forth between it and the cash register so much I didn't have time to wipe the sweat from my forehead or check whether a tray was still hot. I got burned every shift. All my co-workers did. One of them started carrying aloe on her, because if we didn't treat the burns quickly, they'd bubble up into blisters that scarred and left dark yellow pus stains all over our uniforms. I earned $7.25 an hour, before taxes. About three hours for twenty dollars.

▲

You owe me, Mikey texted me the next morning. *You didn't finish lol.*

I was asleep when his message came in. It was the first thing I saw when I woke up. I flung my phone away from me and buried my head under a pillow.

Owe him? What about anything that happened on New Year's made him think I'd do it again? And for free? Even if I was interested, where could that possibly lead? He was not coming out. We were not going to be boyfriends, holding hands at the mall and sipping milkshakes out of the same straw. I wanted to be accepting of his "journey" and be careful with his baby gay feelings, but what about mine? Him using me? He was lucky I hadn't cussed him out when he kissed me. I racked my brain for a response that would be sensitive, yet definitive.

Sorry, I said. *I don't really do that. It was just a one-time thing.*

A few minutes later, he wrote back: *haha sure.*

▲

I got into the University of Central Florida on a full ride paid for by the state.

After getting expelled freshman year of high school, it felt like a miracle. Filling out applications, I'd worried that colleges wouldn't take me seriously. Now, I had to buy a car (To get to campus! A forty-five-minute drive from home.), a laptop (To take notes! What would I need to remember?), figure out what to study (So many options! Who do you even ask for help with these things?). I majored in marketing first, because it sounded fun, taking clients to martini lunches and designing ad campaigns, then I switched to business, because it was vaguer so I imagined it'd be easier to get a job later, then public relations, because PR kids dressed well and seemed to have their shit together, then TV production, because people in TV had to be rolling in money, before finally landing in creative writing.

By then, no matter what I studied, something told me I'd wind up working in food or retail anyway. I had the kind of face that half the time I went into clothing stores, someone would tap me on the shoulder to ask me if we had their size in the back. Little things like that added up. Arriving late to an advertising midterm because my car broke down on the way to class, the professor refusing to give me an exam in front of everyone. No tardies. My academic advisor, returning from a trip to Miami, launching into a tirade about no one speaking English in America anymore. The idea of asking her for a recommendation letter.

I kept looking for a major where I wouldn't have to defend

myself. Writing was the closest to that I found. Whenever I considered studying something more practical, my bottled-up frustrations came out in angry inner monologues. "People like *you* get to make art too!" I'd hype myself up in the shower. "You can't let *them* decide what you do!" I'd pace in circles around my bedroom. "You have to correct the *lies* they're telling about us! This is your *responsibility*!" It was self-aggrandizement, but I needed to self-aggrandize. I was desperate to be big.

"You're a writer!" I'd say, as if it were already true. And I'd keep going like that, until I believed I didn't have a choice.

▲

After New Year's, I'd hoped things would return to normal between Mikey and me. That we could go back to nodding and waving at school from a polite distance like we used to. Pretend we were acquaintances, just two kids who had met volunteering at the library, to meet the requisite community service hours for scholarships. But a line had been crossed. His texts didn't ease up over the months. *Free 2night?* And *Sup cutie!* And *Tease.* Each of them created a deeper rift between us. It wasn't the idea of us hooking up that bothered me; it was his refusal to accept no for an answer. Eventually I stopped replying, and by the time we graduated, we'd grown apart.

I still saw him, though, on occasion. He went to UCF too. He'd be waiting in line at Huey Magoo's. Or coming out of a building, nose buried in a statistics book. A part of me would want to talk to him, I don't know why. A masochistic impulse to be a mentor to him or something, like I would have liked to have. I never did. He seemed busy, and I didn't exactly have any big gay lessons to impart to anyone. What was I going to say? Don't mess around with DL dudes?

▲

My last year of undergrad, a friend invited me to join a burlesque troupe with him. They were an alternative troupe, which only meant that they didn't care what I looked like or that I couldn't dance as long as I could be entertaining somehow. Stripping in a furry thong with a bald cap on, or in a grape costume made of purple balloons I popped with a cigarette. I wasn't confident enough in myself to rely on *sexiness*, to think I could charge for that. But no matter how I dressed up or what I did, I always ended up naked, dollars scattered by my feet.

▲

I'd been working in the men's suits department at JCPenney a little over two months. One night after the store closed, I entered the fitting rooms to pick up the clothes customers left behind. When I reached the final stall, I found a crumpled white dress shirt shoved into a corner by the mirror. I bent over to add it to the pile in my arms, and then I saw it, swaddled inside the shirt's fabric: a piece of shit. I gagged and stumbled backward into the hallway, dropping all the clothes onto the floor. *Nope. Hell no. Not for eight dollars an hour.* I was halfway to the exit when I stopped. It was the thought of Olga—one of my co-workers—clocking in in the morning and having to clean the mess up herself. I couldn't. She'd brought me a home-made cake for my birthday once. Back in the fitting room, I scrubbed the carpet with my head down and my arm pressed to my nose, avoiding my reflection in the mirror. *Fucking Olga.* That cake was delicious.

▲

The years pass. I learn why my mom's feet hurt. Why her back hurt. I'm depressed, and my diet sucks, except when I work at restaurants, and then I eat okay, but I stink. I work at Barnes & Noble, Universal Studios, a magazine, a call center. I work as a substitute teacher, as an administrative assistant. My manager makes a homophobic joke I ignore. Does he know? I intern at Telemundo. A cameraman asks me about Jesus a lot. He must know. This gig pays me in pizza, another in exposure. I'm thrilled about a twenty-five-cent raise. My friends all Venmo each other the same emergency twenty dollars over and over. I will never retire because I bought an iced coffee. I keep falling asleep driving home from my closing shifts at the Gap. Everybody is freaking out about Black Friday, Christmas, Brazilian January, when all the tourists come to Orlando to stock up on brand names. There is never enough time. I'm always running late to train a seventeen-year-old on how to use a cash register. I need three customers to sign up for a credit card or they'll cut my hours. I wake up smiling maniacally, asking the air if it'd like fries or a Coke with its order. My laundry lives in a pile at the edge of my bed, and that, more than anything, makes me so bitter, because I spend eight hours a day folding other people's clothes.

▲

After the Pulse shooting, I left Florida to go to California for a writing master's degree program. I wasn't thinking far ahead when I applied. About how I'd support my mom in her old age. Career options. It was something I'd heard classmates in my undergrad creative writing classes say they were planning to do; I hadn't imagined what I'd do if they accepted me; I just wanted to see if I'd get in, so that during my shifts at work, I could have something to fantasize about, what it would have been like . . .

Then forty-nine queer Latinx people in Orlando had their lives stolen from them. I couldn't stop crying or blacking out every other night. The thought of staying in Florida at my job at the Flip Flop Shop scared me more than starting over on the other side of the country. The program said they'd pay me $2,000 a month to teach, more than I'd made anywhere else. My professors were frank: There were not many university teaching positions after graduating. Very few writers could support themselves without one. But I hadn't really been able to support myself as it was. So I took the offer.

For three years, I tried to put together a book about queer joy and belonging, although most days since I'd arrived in California, I felt neither of those things. The clock was ticking. I drowned it out with the monologue: "You can't let them win!

You have to show them our lives aren't all suffering! This is bigger than just you!"

▲

I had a friend who was a supervising attorney at a nonprofit law center that served immigrant youth in New York, where I moved with my unfinished manuscript after receiving my MFA. She said I was a shoo-in for any of the entry-level positions her job was hiring for. The center was staffed by nearly all non-Latinx people, a major issue considering many of their clients only spoke Spanish. I was skeptical, but my friend said there was health insurance, dental. What would it hurt? Besides, I was getting too old to be googling "How to make money quick???"

The law center provided more than legal services for their clients. They also took the immigrant youth on field trips. Once, before my friend had suggested I apply, I agreed to help her chaperone a group of Central American children to a museum. We saw a new Latin American art exhibit. We cracked jokes about all the parrots. When the tour guide asked us for one fun fact about our cultures, I told them about La Gigantona, the twenty-foot-tall puppet who twirls down the streets in Nicaragua dancing with her short, big-headed sidekick, El Enano Cabezón. "I know them!" one of the kids said. I think I was more excited than he was. I shook hands with my friend's co-workers, women named Kathy, Cheryl. I referenced the trip to the museum on my application. Look, I hoped that would say, I basically already worked for you.

When I didn't hear back, my friend broke it to me that they'd hired someone with more experience and sent me a link to another job opening. She'd wanted to maintain some professional distance last time, but now she said she'd personally ensure my résumé was at the top of the pile. We spent two days on my cover letter. I talked up my master's degree. My family's immigration story. Again, my Spanish fluency. I cringed as I typed "This would be more than a job to me," realizing in that moment that it was the truth. Who was I?

I couldn't think of the last time I'd wanted to work somewhere so badly. Every other job I'd had was disposable. Because most paid minimum wage, whenever a manager threw a tantrum or I couldn't get an important date off, I simply applied somewhere else, knowing there were plenty of other places that would take me. Jobs came and went. It didn't make any difference to me whether I was passing out mesh bags or menus. But I could see myself at the law center for years. I could be useful, capable. I'd make sure they didn't regret hiring me. I went online and picked out a nice pair of shoes to buy if they called me for an interview.

A week passed. Two months. I applied to be a tutor, an editor, a librarian, a flight attendant, a bookseller. Nothing. *Whatever,* I told myself, *it would've been boring there anyway.*

▲

The next time it happened out of nowhere. I was out in Brooklyn. This cute guy messaged me on Grindr. We exchanged pics. With that smooth chest, those thick thighs, I figured half the dudes on the grid were probably blowing up his inbox. *Let's meet up,* I said, locking it down quick. He sent me his address, a twenty-minute walk away. On my way there, all of a sudden he remembered he had a friend in town staying with him. Did I, um, mind if the friend watched?

The fuck? was my first thought.

But I'd already started walking.

He can for fifty dollars, I told him, curious how he'd answer, since we were apparently saying anything we felt like.

A gray text bubble materialized on-screen. Three blinking dot dot dots.

Cool, he replied. *Give me ten minutes. Gotta run to an ATM.*

▲

The call center had a system in place where you had to swipe a key card whenever you went in and out of the bathroom. It was so they could measure how much time you spent inside. At the end of the week, you had a meeting with your supervisor where they said things like "Was it an emergency?" "Couldn't you hold it?" "Have you tried drinking less water?" If you improved, they rewarded you with coupons you could trade in for soda and candy, like at school.

▲

This guy was visiting from Pakistan. He messaged me talking about how he was on his last trip abroad before getting married and he'd never done anything before, how he just wanted to try once, that he didn't know when he'd get another opportunity. Please? $150 for a massage.

▲

At the gay bar in Hell's Kitchen where I worked as a cocktail server, a group of twinks ordered a round of tequila sodas. When the drinks were ready, I lifted the tray over my head and elbowed my way through the packed crowd on the dance floor, trying to get to where the boys were sitting, when out of nowhere a hand grabbed my crotch. Squeezed it. I flinched, and through what had to have been divine intervention, regained my balance before the drinks slipped to the floor. Nobody heard me yelling over the music, "Who did that?!" Everyone kept dancing. The air smelled of poppers. My stupid dick was hard. "Who grabbed me?!" I searched the crowd, my nostrils flaring. "No thanks, I'm good," a voice beside me answered. "I already have a drink."

▲

Another friend hooked me up with a job working gay sex parties at clubs in Manhattan, where he said I could make $300 to $400 a night for a few hours of taking tickets at the door, some light cleaning. Making sure everything was running smoothly. The one catch was I couldn't hook up with the guests, he warned me. *They fire you if they even see you flirting. Seriously.*

For $400, I told him, *I promise I can go a night without having sex with a stranger.*

At the first party, I was like an intern, eager to impress. I showed up to the small gay bar near the studio where they filmed *The Wendy Williams Show* half an hour early, wearing all black like my new boss texted me to. Within minutes, he shoved sixty dollars into my hand and sent me on an errand to go buy "a bucket of lube" and "two DVDs of interracial porn." I got flustered seeing the prices at the sex shop—sixty dollars wouldn't cover it—and tried explaining to the cashier that I couldn't get fired, I'd just started. When she gave me a 10 percent industry discount, I felt like when I worked at Auntie Anne's and traded pretzels for ice cream with the Häagen-Dazs employees. "Thank you!" I burst out, smiling.

That first night was slow. By ten o'clock, there were only three dudes standing around in jockstraps, a couple more having sex in the back room. A lot of curious guys who'd seen the ad on Twitter stuck their heads in through the front door of the bar, took one look at the neon lights pirouetting across the empty dance floor, and left. My friend said most of my money would come from tips. I was beginning to think the $400 had been an exaggeration. But at least the job was chill, and I had a fifteen-dollar-an-hour, under-the-table base pay for refilling the condom bowl and mopping up lube. It wasn't the worst thing. I'd cleaned up shit at JCPenney for less.

By eleven o'clock, my boss was sweating. Pacing. Anxiously eyeing the door. He'd anticipated a larger crowd and had even hired a porn star to put on a show for them at midnight. I could see the fear flashing across his face. There was no way he'd earned enough to pay for it all.

Finally, a group of guys walked in.

"Wanna take a break?" my boss asked me as the men looked past us to the dance floor, and then to each other, disappointed. "I can handle it up here. Go to the back room. Have fun."

I was confused. Was this a trick? Everyone back there was fucking. It's not like I could sit beside them and eat the granola bar I brought for my fifteen. What did he mean, *have fun?*

"My friend said you didn't like when we hooked up with guests?" I asked.

"Nah, don't worry about that," my boss answered, then circled behind the men and nudged them my way. "You got your tickets, right? My boy here will show you around."

They stared me up and down.

"The short one is cute, huh?" my boss whispered into my ear. "Show them the back," he said, pushing me toward them. "Come on."

It took me a moment to understand.

"Oh," I answered.

Years later, this is the part that gets me. That I didn't even think to say no. How fast it all happened. Wasn't I supposed to feel offended? Ashamed? Somewhere along the line, I imagine I would have at least been surprised. But after a while, all the jobs I'd ever had and what I felt about them blurred together. *You can't sit. You can't lean. You can't do that to your appearance. You must do this with your body.*

Don't get me wrong. I'm not saying it's the same. There are people who would rather starve. What I'm saying is I wasn't one of them.

At other parties, he'd brag to customers about my back rubs. He'd say, "Some sexy guys came in earlier. Here's a little extra."

He'd say, "Go over there. Make them feel welcome." Once or twice they actually were sexy, only at the parties for the convenience. More often I was relieved it was dark, so I could think about my exes. It was their lips on my neck, their fingers sliding into my briefs. They'd pull my hair or shove me against a wall, and it'd be scary for a second, but then I'd remember there were other people around and shake it off. Afterward they'd lay on the sweetness. "Let me take care of you, Pa." "I can spoil you."

Fine, I always wanted to say. *Spoil me.* Just to see the horror on their faces.

▲

The last time I saw Mikey, he was on TV. Sitting in the front row at a Beyoncé concert. He must have been on-screen a dozen times before I recognized him, screaming his head off wearing a sequined blazer with a tiny silver bow tie and everything. And it all flooded back: driving out of the swamp listening to Madonna, his crappy car, my perfume, the afternoon we were reshelving books at the library and he'd said, *Let me get your number, in case I can't make it one day and need you to let someone know.* The familiar impulse to reach out seized me. To tell him I was proud he'd finally made it, that we should get together to catch up. I was scrolling through my contacts when he reappeared on-screen. Mikey! I put my phone down and watched. In the front row! Looking like a guest judge on *RuPaul's Drag Race.* Made it? I shook my head, grinning as he sang along to Beyoncé. Who did I think I was? This bitch. He was further ahead than I was.

▲

I did so well at the parties my boss spoke to the manager of a gay bathhouse in Queens for me. It was on the second floor of a furniture store, across the street from a gas station. *Bathhouse* is the word the owner used to describe it, but there was no bath component to the place. In reality, it was a few rooms with rubber-block beds, a long, dark corridor with private nooks, and a common area with a leather swing and some couches and a movie screen for porn. In an alternate universe, it could've been one of those religious haunted houses where you hear gay people crying in pain and being whipped by demons, Jesus waiting to hug you if you made it out. Black curtains blocked the sun from entering through the windows wrapping around the building. They gave everybody who worked there tiny flashlights to see.

My job depended on the shift. I'd either be on the disinfecting team or at the front desk, handing out garbage bags for the men to put their clothes in, double-checking they didn't sneak drugs or hidden cameras in through their socks. I'd only done it twice, but I could already tell disinfecting wasn't worth it. Trying to breathe through the stench of cum and bleach, awkwardly wiping lube handprints off the walls while someone's dad got absolutely railed beside me. It got old fast. But I planned to play up my customer service background so they'd give me a permanent position at the front desk. There, I could kick back, read, get stoned. On Fridays, management ordered the employees pizza. And again, it was all under the table—no taxes.

"There's people who've been working here for years," one of

the guys training me said. We were settled in the reception area during a lull between customers. "The money's nice, but you can't do this shit forever, man. No health insurance. Can't get a loan from the bank if you want a house. You don't want to be here when you're forty. You get used to the money, you get comfortable, stop going to school. I see it all the time. This job's easy, but don't get trapped."

I thought about the manuscript on my computer, and what I'd been trying to convince myself of for a while now. That there was a point to all this. That I was doing something.

"Thanks," I told him. "I won't."

"All right, long as you know." He leaned back and laughed. "Next guy is all *you*."

7

MY BOYFRIEND,
HIS LOVER, AND ME

We were out to dinner at a fancy Mediterranean restaurant when my boyfriend Diego told me about his famous lover.

At the risk of sounding desperate, Diego wasn't technically my "boyfriend," though in my defense, we'd seen each other every single day for the previous two months, from our first date at the gay bar a block from my old apartment in Sunset Park, till the day before, when he helped me move to Bed-Stuy, a forty-five-minute train ride to the other end of Brooklyn. If there is a word for the phase in a relationship between when you begin dating and when you start using the more serious terminology—*boyfriend, partner, situation-ship*—that was what we were.

But technically, Diego's lover was not his "lover" either, because they did not have sex. "We're just affectionate," Diego clarified. I assume he shared this generous bit of insight into their arrangement in response to the dazed look in my eyes, since I hadn't yet said a word.

Up until that second, the two of us only having enough money to split an appetizer portion of baba ganoush had seemed kind of romantic. We were both in our mid-twenties. Struggling artists (him: a painter, me: a writer). Trying to make it in New York. Our hunger had the potential to be a charming anecdote later, when we made it far enough in our respective careers that we could look back and laugh, as if it were something that belonged to other people in faraway lives. Now, however, hearing his lover-but-not-quite-lover's name, our future together, and the charm that came with it, vanished.

You see, his lover was also an artist. One who had, by any measure, made it.

In his mid-fifties, he was one of those gay celebrities who is somehow good at everything, with a career spanning from Broadway to TV and film. His lover was so famous that when Diego told me his name (I'll call him C), my first thought was *Oh no, I love that guy.*

Not *Oh no, my boyfriend, who I think I love, is dating someone else.*

But *Oh no, I love my boyfriend's lover.*

C might as well have been Rihanna, he was so universally adored. I wasn't even sure if I was allowed to be mad. I mean, it's *Rihanna.* Of course I couldn't ask Diego to break it off. It's *C,* that one famous gay guy everyone likes, a fact about him that, coupled with his whiteness, felt like undeniable proof of his greed. He had all those fans, all that money. He probably owned an island somewhere, or at least a Segway. Did he really need to have my boyfriend, too?

What happened, Diego explained, was that he started seeing me around the same time that he started seeing him. He figured he'd keep going on dates with the two of us while he decided who he liked more. After getting to know each of us, it turned out he liked both.

"I'm sorry I didn't tell you sooner," Diego said, staring into our plate of fifteen-dollar mashed eggplant. "I was going to, but I just kept pushing and pushing it."

I didn't know how to respond. Was I supposed to accept his apology with grace and poise? Or did the situation call for me to react like a scorned woman in a telenovela, throw my drink in his face and accuse him of being a maldito sin vergüenza? I took a long sip of water and told myself to be chill. To let the news sit for a moment before I did something I'd regret.

But the more I thought about it, the less what he was telling me made sense. Just the night before, we'd been lying in my bed after a second round of sex.

"I've never been with anyone like you," he'd said as he reached for our gold chains coiled together on my nightstand, where we'd flung them because the crosses kept getting tangled while he was on top of me. "With every other Latinx guy I've dated there's been something, I don't know, missing, but this feels so *right*."

I understood him completely. I'd dated other Latinx men, but there was always something off about those relationships. Either they felt a little too orchestrated ("I love your brown body against mine," a man told me once on our second date, like we were a matching skirt and blouse), or there were other strange power dynamics that put me on edge.

When I dated Latinx men who didn't speak Spanish or were of the blond-haired, blue-eyed variety, I got the feeling they were using me to prove something about their own identities, as if they were playing Seven Degrees of Separation from Sofía Vergara and I was a critical link.

Then, with Latinx men who were recent immigrants to the United States, I was too Americanized. I may have been born in Miami—basically a mini Latin America—and spent every summer of my childhood in Nicaragua, but they were right, our experiences were different.

I suppose the real issue was with trying to connect through the overly broad identity tag Latinidad, which pretends that millions of people across race, class, and country are the same simply because we have roots in nations that were once conquered. Growing up in Orlando as the child of a Central American woman, with zero other Nicaraguan kids in sight, claiming a spot under the wider Latinx umbrella helped me find a place among children who, if they had nothing else in common with me, also watched Telemundo at home; in that way, clinging to the flawed myth of magical Latinx unity helped me feel a little less alone. As an adult, as I began to see how much discrimination exists within Latinx communities, I became more skeptical of that unity, yet my desire to be with others who understood what living in diaspora was like remained.

Diego had a similar experience to mine. Though he was born in Mexico, he spent most of his life in Arizona, where his parents immigrated when he was a child, as a DACA recipient. Both of us were raised on Fabuloso, *Sábado Gigante*, and Takis.

Perhaps it was coming of age as children of Spanish-speaking immigrants, if not Latinidad, that bonded me to him. Whatever it was, we were, like he said, oddly *right* together. Like mango slices and salt, like our love story was global. Our families' migrations had ended with me sitting across a table from him in Brooklyn, surrounded by people speaking Turkish, the two of us talking about some pasty white dude who couldn't stay in his lane.

"I'm so confused," I finally found the nerve to say. "Are you poly?"

There were a thousand other questions racing through my mind, but finding out whether he planned on ever choosing between me and C seemed most urgent.

"No. I'm not really into polyamory."

"Well, are you into me?" was my second question.

It felt stupid to ask. Of course he was. Though, actually, I wasn't so sure. C was Rihanna, and I couldn't even afford my own entrée.

"Yes," he said, squeezing my hand. "I like you. A lot."

My third question was going to be: *When did you even have time to see someone else? We've been together every single day for the last two months!*

The fourth: *Were you with him on days you were with me? Did you leave my bed to go off and be "affectionate" with him?*

The fifth: *What do you mean by "affectionate?" Were we not that? What about that time we got stoned and watched* Los Espookys *until three a.m., and I held you as you slept, adjusting my body to your breaths, and when I woke up you were holding me? Or that day I let myself text you that I missed you despite how corny it felt to type those words out, and you showed up to my job with a paper bag of really bad flan from the deli? Do you know that when I told my co-workers you were coming, I said you were my boyfriend, because what else was I supposed to call you, my "guy-I-see-every-day-who-brings-me-flan"?*

And underlying all those questions was the one I could have never brought myself to ask: *Why don't you just pick me?*

I swallowed them all. I knew what I needed to know: he was here with me now. He planned on choosing one of us eventually. He was holding *my* hand.

Sure, C was Rihanna, but he was almost twice Diego's age, and *they* didn't have all those things in common *we* did. *They* didn't even have sex, whereas when *we* fucked, it was as if our bodies were designed for each other. *We* understood, in our DNA, where to lick, press, squeeze, kiss, which trails to follow. *We* were Rottweilers. *They* were what? "Affectionate." Oh, please.

C, I thought, would be another charming anecdote later, just like these years as starving artists. A decade from now I'd turn over to Diego in bed and whisper, "Remember when you chose me over Rihanna?" We'd laugh, then I'd get up and make us coffee and eggs.

I am a memoirist. There is nothing I want more than a happy ending.

"Okay," I said, and pushed our dinner over to him so he could have the rest.

"Okay?" he asked.

"It's fine. Just . . . don't tell him about me," I added.

I didn't understand then why I needed the discretion, though I do now. If C knew we were in competition, he might try to woo Diego with all the resources I didn't have. This way, at least there'd be a modicum of fairness.

"Okay," he agreed.

That would have been a horrifying enough place to end the night except, on the train to my apartment, C joined us for the ride. His smug face was plastered on ads all along the train car, promotion for his latest project. The cameo was too coinciden-tal, too hellish; I wouldn't believe it if I read it in a story, yet there he was, glowing in the overhead lights. Diego looked at me like I was a stray kitten he was deciding whether to feed. By some impossible force of will, my heart did not leap out of my chest, my cheeks did not redden. I might've even smiled.

Don't, I wanted to tell him. *Don't look at me like that. I'm not famous, but I am great. I make you laugh. I make you cum. You said yourself that we're right. Please don't pity me. Pick me.*

Two months before that night at the restaurant, I met Diego on Grindr. I'd only been in New York a few weeks and was work-ing as a cashier at a Mexican restaurant. When I wasn't behind the counter up-charging guac, I was at home, scrolling through dating apps: like my profile said, "Looking." Diego's photo caught my eye. He reminded me of the cholos I knew from Southern California, where I'd lived for the previous three years. In his grainy mirror selfie, only the neck of his plaid shirt was buttoned. His jet-black hair was slicked back in a greaser style, one tendril dangling over his forehead. On his face, he wore a smile I would come to know well; more of a smirk really, his lips raised higher on one side, like he was keeping a good secret.

We messaged back and forth a bit. It was a little past midnight on a Thursday, but he wanted to get a drink.

There's a gay bar a block from my apartment, I replied. *Xstasy.* Had he ever heard of it?

Yeah, he wrote back. *I love the vibe there.*

With those words, I was instantly smitten.

When I first moved to the city, the queer white woman I was subletting a room from told me there was a gay bar nearby, but that it was "sketchy." Naturally, it was the first place I visited after unpacking. There was nothing particularly seedy about it. It was a predominantly Latinx bar that attracted a fun crowd of queer construction workers. On slow summer afternoons, the bartender described Stephen King novels to me between rounds of cheap drinks. I'd been suggesting Xstasy to dates as a litmus test ever since. If they said no and recommended we go to one of the snobby gay bars in Hell's Kitchen, I knew we weren't a match.

That night, I put on a pair of tight blue jeans and walked over. Diego lived a train ride away so I arrived first. While I waited, I made small talk with the bartender, who bemoaned that the current season of *RuPaul's Drag Race* would soon be over, meaning the regulars that came in on Thursdays—me included—would likely disappear. I ordered a shot.

To RuPaul.

"What are you gonna do on Thursdays now?" he asked.

I shrugged. "I'm seeing this guy tonight. Maybe I'll fall in love."

He poured me another round of tequila.

"See you next Thursday," the bartender teased.

By the time Diego showed up, I was buzzed enough to tell him he looked dorky in his khaki pants and V-neck sweater. This costume was so different from the character I'd formed of him based on his pictures, but he was cute nonetheless.

"Shut up!" He blushed and shot me that I-have-a-secret smirk.

I wonder now if he'd come from a date with C, at a Broadway show or an art gallery, somewhere he had to dress up for.

"I didn't know what *you* were going to wear," he said.

Our conversation slipped in and out of Spanish and English. We talked about *Drag Race,* pet chickens we had as kids, his graduate art school program, all the while drifting closer to each other. When there was only an inch left between us, we moved over to the small dance floor the size of a bodega where a DJ spun feverish house music though we were the only ones there. Diego steered me into a dark corner, pushed my back against a wall. A stream of smoke from a fog machine curled by our feet like a cat's tail. His mouth was cold and sweet from the rum and Cokes we'd had. I held his face close to mine, and for a few seconds we didn't kiss exactly, though our lips were pressed together. It was more like we were breathing into each other.

"¿Quieres pasar la noche conmigo?" he asked. *Wanna come over?*

Outside, we walked toward the 25th Street R train with our fingers interlocked. At that hour of the night, the trains came further and further apart, so we took our time, stopping every few steps to make out, or laugh about something that probably wasn't that funny. There was an abandoned brownstone on the way to the station with a small garden out front that I really loved. It was just a little patch of wild grass, guarded by a gnome, but for some reason it reminded me of my neighborhood in Orlando, of family. We looked into it for a couple of minutes. I let myself indulge in a fantasy of what it'd be like to fix the place up, live in it with him or someone like him, when suddenly Diego turned to me and asked, "Do you know what's the worst thing?"

"No, what's the worst thing?" I grinned.

"When you get to the station just as the train is taking off. And you're like standing there thinking, *Fuck, if I'd only left like* thirty *seconds sooner, I would have caught it*. Especially this late, when you have to wait twenty minutes for the next one."

"Yeah, I hate that."

"It's the worst."

"Let's catch it then," I said, grabbing his hand, and we took off running.

A few weeks after Diego told me about their relationship, C made another cameo. He was an A-list celebrity at my newest job: taking reservations for a group of luxury restaurants in

SoHo. I'd quit the Mexican restaurant because my new manager promised I would have a lot of downtime that I could use to read or write, an opportunity I couldn't pass on, though I mostly spent my shifts brooding. The job consisted of taking guests' phone calls; depending on how ridiculous their request was ("I need a table for fifteen people in five minutes!"), I would look up their number in our database of regular diners and determine whether we could accommodate them.

The database contained thousands of profiles. On a whim one day, I typed C's name in. He popped up right away. To be on the A-list, actually, was the worst-best thing you could be. Our guests were either unrated (they only dined with us a few times) or rated from A (relatively famous/spent a lot of money) to triple A (extremely famous/probably wouldn't even deign to *touch* money). A-listers didn't really get anything special. Just my boyfriend.

Next to C's name was his phone number, and next to my first impulse to look him up was this psychotic idea: *Call him.*

I didn't, but it became a favorite masochistic hobby of mine to pass the time wondering how a conversation between the two of us might go.

Hey, I would start. *You don't know me, but I know you. We have someone in common: Diego. We're both kind of dating him. Before you hang up, I know this is crazy, I swear I do. But please, hear me out. How can I put this to you so you'll understand?*

Dating is so hard for gay people, right? Well, it's a little harder when you're Latinx. There's a lot of culturally specific shame and machismo and religious and family baggage we carry, and it's just so much easier to be with other Latinx people who know what that's like. But more than that trauma crap, I like Diego. So much.

And it's weird, but I think my mom would like him. We get each other's references, we speak the same languages, and the sex we have, phew, girl, all of it is just so good. That means something to him, I know it does, or he would have left me already.

Okay, you guys are "affectionate," but come on. You have so much! You have money. You're a celebrity. You'll find someone else. I know it's up to him to choose, but it's not really a fair match, is it? You can introduce him to cool people, open doors for him in the art world I can't. I get that he should pick you. I'm actually a huge fan. But you're also a famous white guy, like what the fuck kind of "Amor Prohibido" bullshit are you trying to pull? If you don't know what I'm talking about, that's exactly the point! Y'all look wild together. You're not gonna end up with him! So how about you save both of us time and stay away from my man, you little—

Around this point in the fantasy, my co-workers would notice me silently fuming. Before they got too annoyed with me for ignoring our endless call queue, I'd close out C's profile and go back to work: helping rich people get whatever they wanted, as long as they mattered enough.

To be clear: I have broken up with men for way less than having some dude on the side.

This one guy had a weird smell no one noticed but me, which I interpreted as a warning from my primal animal instincts that we weren't biologically compatible. Another guy started wearing this scary Halloween store goth choker all the time. It was part of a costume, but then he never took it off. Rather than ask him to change his style for me, I suggested we see other people. Listen, I do have boundaries; I won't settle for just anybody. *Diego,* though. He could have worn a zoot suit and smelled like sausages, and I would have loved him the same.

I didn't want to fall in love with him, not while he was still deciding between us, but one night, against my better judgment, it just happened.

That night, he'd invited me to his apartment for dinner. We were holed up in his tiny kitchen; him cutting up onions and cilantro for ceviche, me drinking glass after glass of Two Buck Chuck. Juan Luis Guerra played on my phone. "Burbujas de Amor," a song with cheesy lyrics that had become a private joke to us for some reason I can't remember. It's about a man who wants to be a fish, so he can blow bubbles in a woman's "tank."

"You don't want help?" I'd asked him.

"Don't worry about it." He smiled, keeping his eyes on the vegetables he was finishing cutting. "I like cooking for you."

I nuzzled the back of his neck with my nose and sang along: "Quisiera ser un pez . . ."

As I held him, I felt both dizzy and giddy thinking about how this domestic scene looked nothing like the heteronormative relationship models I'd been brought up with. He was the top. I was the bottom. I was supposed to be making him dinner, and he was supposed to be nursing a beer on the couch. Yet here we were, creating something new.

After dinner, we went out for a walk. It was a weekend night, nearing the end of summer, and everyone was out enjoying the last bits of warmth before the sidewalks would be covered in snow. Reggaeton and banda mingled in the breeze as we strolled through his neighborhood, our skin glistening with sweat. On our way to the bodega for paletas to cool off, we passed a group of older women drinking out of Solo cups in the small patch of concrete in front of their apartment New Yorkers call "yards." They slurred their words as they waxed on from their lawn chairs about their lazy, good-for-nothing husbands.

"¡Mi panzón se queda sentado en frente de la tele todo el maldito día!" one howled to the others. Her friends nodded their heads solemnly. "¡Pero lo amo!"

My fat husband sits at home watching TV all day, but I love him!

Diego and I both cracked up. They sounded exactly like our tías at family parties. Had he been anyone else, I might have felt self-conscious about laughing. I would have been annoyed if a non-Latinx guy thought they were funny before I got the chance to translate what they'd said (was he laughing *at* them?), annoyed that I would have had to translate in the first place, which would invariably make their conversation lose some of its magic. But Diego just got it. No need to explain. I wrapped my arm around his waist and patted his belly as we walked on.

"Mi panzón," I whispered.

The two of us giggled.

"Mi panzón es un pinche boludo," he picked up after me,

mimicking their high-pitched voices, then kissed my forehead and hugged me closer. "Pero lo amo. ¡Ay dios, lo amo!"

I knew, right then, that I would ride this out wherever it went.

Not long after that night, the universe sent good news and bad news.

The bad news was that Diego's roommates, a straight couple, decided that they all of a sudden needed more space and privacy. They gave him one month to find somewhere else to live. The timing couldn't have been worse. Diego worked for a nonprofit group that operated in the summer, taking children to cultural events all over the city. With the season coming to an end, he'd lost his main source of income. Finding another job would be complicated because of his resident status. Under Trump, would DACA even exist much longer?

The good news for him—which was actually more bad news for me—was that C had just been cast in a TV show that would be shooting out of town for the next couple of months. He offered Diego his very nice apartment in Manhattan, rent-free. They would technically be living together, though C would be in another state. Diego broke this to me over text while I was at work. Apparently he'd confided to C that he was planning to sleep in the closet-size art studio his graduate school provided students. C miraculously stepped in to save the day. I couldn't believe this was happening. This motherfucker was like, gentrifying my love life!

Obviously I couldn't tell Diego, *No, don't take the amazing rent-free apartment. I know you don't have money right now for another security deposit and first and last months' rent, but it would make me more comfortable if you slept in a closet.*

I also couldn't tell him to move in with me. We'd only dated for three and a half months. I'm not crazy.

Offering a whole-ass apartment was the kind of grand gesture I could never compete with. For the first time, it seemed possible to me that I might actually lose Diego. I'm sure C had a thousand and one wonderful qualities that made him more than the white savior I'd reduced him to in my mind, but I thought: *I am going to lose the love of my life because I am poor.*

Somehow that was easier to stomach than the other possibility: that I might lose Diego because he simply preferred C, and the fact that he was rich had nothing to do with it. At least I could delude myself into thinking one day I would have money. But for him to *like* C more—like his stories, his lips, his affection more—what was I supposed to do with that?

Wow, I wrote back after an hour. *That's so generous.*

Diego was going to make me pancakes. He showed up to my apartment before noon, his backpack brimming with groceries he could afford because he didn't have to pay rent. I greeted him barefoot, wearing a T-shirt he'd left behind some night, and kissed him on the cheek while he unpacked a bag of flour and bottles of syrup and oil on my kitchen table. As soon as he finished, he stared at the ingredients for a long time, then, weirdly, put all of it back into his bag.

"I have to tell you something," he said.

He glanced at my bare walls and at the small sofa tucked into a corner of the room, like he was taking in my apartment for the first time. I saw it through his eyes, cringing inside.

"But not in here," he sighed. "I don't want to leave any bad energy in here. Can we go for a walk?"

"Sure," I said, playing it off, though I knew nothing good could come from those words. I slunk into my bedroom and put on a pair of sneakers. "Just like, around the block?"

"Yeah," he said. "That's fine."

He slung his backpack over his shoulder, a small gesture that made my blood run cold. We stepped out of my apartment, walking down the hallway one behind the other, instead of side by side. He apologized about not responding to a text I'd sent him the night before.

"It's because I was sort of with someone," he said.

I couldn't see his face. Thankfully, he couldn't see mine. My cheeks must have cycled through every possible color.

Out on the sidewalk, I wanted so badly to be chill.

"Yeah?" I said as we walked, hoping it'd be nothing, that he'd tell me he was at the movies with a friend or something.

"I'm thinking of doing this thing where I have sex—for like, money," he said. "I mean, I did. That's what I was doing last night."

The minutes melted away as we walked on in silence.

I was still new to the neighborhood. Nothing looked familiar. I gaped around and couldn't remember how we'd gotten to where we were, a quiet park; how I'd gotten here, in my life. When I was very little, I used to think that by twenty-seven, I'd be a doctor with three kids and a minivan. What I had was a dead-end, minimum-wage job, a boyfriend who wasn't really my boyfriend, and a handful of published stories I built my identity as a so-called writer around. I felt like that Robert Frost poem, looking at the fork in the road I could've taken, and the one I did. The truth was neither of them seemed all that appealing.

"Oh," I said.

"Yeah," he responded.

I tried to iron out my thoughts: I didn't believe sex work was immoral. I'd done it; many of my friends had, too. He *did* need the money. Maybe, my mind worked double time to justify, this could be like that night in the kitchen, another opportunity for us to define what our relationship would look like.

"With who?" I asked.

"Some guy from Grindr," he said. "Does it matter who?"

It did. In my ape brain, it absolutely did. I wanted the guy to be two hundred years old. I wanted Diego to say he'd thought of me the whole time. I knew this wasn't fair, but I wanted it.

"Were you safe?"

He dropped his eyes to his sneakers. "No."

I clung to that. I couldn't be angry that he was dating someone famous, or that he was sleeping in another man's apartment, or that he was doing sex work, but that—that was too far.

"Why not?" I asked. "You know how risky that is."

"I . . .," he said. "I don't know. I know. I'm sorry."

My chest deflated. Suddenly, I couldn't bear to argue. I didn't want him to feel guilty, not for doing what he had to do, not even if what he had to do hurt me.

As I stood there deciding what to say to him next, it was not beyond me how easily our story could be summed up with a handful of clichés: the poor children of immigrants, the queer couple doomed to break up over sex, the white knight. Up until then, I'd believed that if I told myself these were just silly stereotypes, they wouldn't get to me—that I could wear my self-awareness like armor. But it was clear to me now just how delusional that line of thinking was.

After all, I was perfectly aware that, if Diego liked me and C the same, it made sense that he should choose the person who could help him most. I was aware that, even if Diego liked me a little bit more, C would still be the smarter pick. I was aware of these things, and yet they didn't protect me. If anything, they left me more vulnerable than ever.

"Do you not want to see me anymore?" I asked him at last.

It was a selfish question. If he chose me, our lives would be a gamble. We might never do more than get stoned and fall asleep together on the couch. For the foreseeable future, we would likely struggle with money. Who knew how much longer we'd be hungry? I wasn't trying to dismiss that there'd be sacrifices, but still, I thought we could be happy. We could figure it out.

Diego stared off at a point far down the street.

"I always do this," he said.

"Do you not want to see me anymore?" I repeated, trying to keep my voice from breaking, because I suspected if he knew how much his answer could devastate me, he'd lie.

He took a deep breath, then, without looking at my face, said, "It's just getting hard to have to consider you."

The words sank into me like a rock.

Okay, Panzón, I thought. *Good for you. Good for choosing you.* I didn't say it, but I meant it. I still do.

I turned around and walked back to my apartment alone, feeling as if I were drowning, unsure if I was even heading in the right direction. Eventually I found my way to my building, pulled myself up the steps, pushed my door open, and collapsed onto the floor of the living room.

Lying on the ground, I felt trapped under the weight of a thousand questions.

The first: *If he came here to break up with you, then why did he bring all those ingredients?*

The second: *Did you do something, between him unpacking his backpack and asking to go on the walk, that made him think you weren't worth it?*

The third: *Did you make a mistake asking him if he didn't want to see you anymore?*

The fourth: *Did you make a mistake meeting him too soon? Would meeting him years from now, when you'd made it, have made a difference, when everything else was so right?*

And underlying all those questions were the ones I could have never brought myself to ask: *Wasn't it? Or is "this feels so right" just something polite people say after sex?*

Hovering a foot above my limp body, my roommate's Siri was plugged into the wall. I wanted to hear someone else feel as pathetic as I did. Adele. Toni Braxton.

"Siri, play a sad song," I whimpered.

But she misheard me, and she played Sisqó's "Thong Song."

As the dramatic, opening violin chords poured out of the speaker, my lips grudgingly curled into a smile, and then I broke out into tears, and then I was laughing and sobbing, my chest heaving, a part of me grateful for Siri's mistake, which felt like a sign of solidarity from the universe, its way of telling me to relax and see that this was all so dumb, so ridiculous.

Another part of me wished the universe would shut the fuck up for once and let me have my misery, because this wasn't funny. I loved him, and that wasn't dumb, that wasn't ridiculous.

Halfway through the song, it occurred to me that the train Diego would have to get on to head back to C's apartment in the city would probably pull up to the station any minute now. It was the only train nearby, the same one I needed to take to go to Xstasy or meet up with a friend who might help me end my pity party. If I wanted to avoid Diego, all I had to do was wait thirty more seconds for it to depart. Then I could pick myself up off the floor, get the next one.

Or I could run, go and try to catch Diego before he left forever, not spend the rest of my life agonizing over what would have happened if I had put my pride aside and fought harder for us. I could have told him to pick me and not just hoped he'd do it on his own.

"You know what's the worst thing?" Diego had asked me the night we met.

I'd been staring at the abandoned brownstone, getting lost in our rom-com life. What I remembered all these months later, as I lay on the floor, is that even after running to the station, we still didn't make it on time. We might as well have lingered a few more minutes outside on the sidewalk, enjoying the night, dreaming.

So for a little while longer I let myself keep laughing and sobbing on the floor. There was no point rushing. We were never going to live there. I was going to miss that train.

8

IMAGES OF RAPTURE

The night before lockdown restrictions began, I went to work. It was March 2020. I'd lived in New York for almost two years by then, and I still wasn't used to winters in the city. The way the bitter, freezing wind slapped me across the face the moment I stepped out of my apartment in Brooklyn; the dull, wet, gray dreariness of it all. That Thursday, I rode the train into Manhattan using the hood of my puffer coat as a pillow, nodding in and out of sleep, too cold and tired to fully process the look of doom in other riders' eyes. I'd already worked a morning shift at my day job, taking reservations for the luxury restaurant group in SoHo, and I had one more shift at my night job before I could go home. If I'd had a choice, I would've stayed in bed hibernating. I would have been more cautious, like the good people on the internet were warning everyone to be. But I needed to make some money.

Forty minutes later I climbed out of the train station and made my way through Hell's Kitchen toward Industry, the gay bar two blocks from Times Square where I'd recently been hired as a cocktail server. My last paycheck from the restaurant group had barely been enough to cover my credit card bills and Metro-Card; with news of Covid-19 circulating through the city, wealthy New Yorkers were eating out less, leading my supervisors to cut my hours in half. I was broke. Desperate. Stealing rolls of toilet paper from my job's supply closet like the dollar I saved would make a difference. Stepping through Industry's heavy wooden doors, I thanked God I had a second source of income, even if it meant I'd have to spend another evening having drunk clients scream their orders at me while I smiled and wiped their spit off of my cheek.

It's fine, I'd been telling myself ever since I read an article that claimed that was how the virus spread. Through respiratory droplets. *Everything's fine. Just don't think about it too much.*

On Thursdays, Industry was usually packed shoulder to shoulder with tourists and Broadway gays, but this night there were only a handful of people seated at the bar. The vibe inside was more tense than it had been all week—the new Dua Lipa disco track piping in through the speakers contrasted sharply with the sad, empty dance floor. Most folks in the city who could afford to quarantine already told their bosses they weren't going in. In the last few days, my co-workers at Industry had gone from speculating about whether the bar would close to making arrangements for what they'd do when it inevitably happened. Restarting their OnlyFans. Sheltering in place with family in Jersey. I started my shift wiping down tables, privately making my own plans. I had one more check coming in from my reservations gig, one from the bar: How long could I stretch my money out, if I needed to? A couple weeks? And then what?

The panic must have shown on my face, because when I went behind the bar to grab some more towels, my favorite bartender, Josh, poured two whiskey shots.

"Bitch, you look like you need this." He thrust one at me.

I downed it quickly, looking around for a manager. "You're not gonna get in trouble?"

"Trouble?" He laughed and poured two more. "Let them say something. They should be happy my ass is even here. Everyone's calling out."

The liquor helped calm my nerves, numbing me enough to keep going. As the hours rolled by, more people began to trickle in, until there were a good dozen seated at the tables surrounding the stage where one of Industry's resident drag queens, Tina Burner, was scheduled to perform later. She'd appeared on *RuPaul's Drag Race* a couple of years earlier—we could always count on her fans to show up to see her.

But by midnight, almost no one new had arrived. The gays who'd been waiting for the show were getting antsy. They'd finished their first and second cocktails and had started chewing on ice cubes, anxiously eyeing one another like they were looking for permission to leave. I swooped in to take their last orders, adding their tips to my mental bank: two dollars here, three dollars there. With each addition, the reality of what I was doing felt more and more absurd. I'd probably take home less than fifty bucks. And maybe Covid. This wasn't worth it, for any of us.

I was at the bar, fetching someone their drink, when the DJ finally welcomed Tina Burner to the stage. Next to me, Josh stopped cutting limes and looked up. "Oh my god," he said, and nudged me with his elbow. I followed his gaze to Tina, who'd emerged through the red velvet curtain onstage backed by the instrumental track of Frank Sinatra's "New York, New York." She slinked up to the microphone wearing a yellow latex gown hugging every inch of her curves. Printed all over it was the word CORONA, in the same font as the beer, a dress she must have already had in her closet from a past corporate event. She winked as we all took her outfit in.

I delivered the drink to the front row, my eyes glued to the stage. "Too soon," someone whispered as I passed their table to go watch the show by the DJ booth. But it really was too soon— the full scale of the pandemic hadn't hit the country yet. It was hard to tell how seriously we were supposed to take it. As I stood there, awkward giggles rippling through the small crowd, I found myself giggling along with everyone else. Tina brought her glossy lips to the mic and sang the hopeful opening lyrics about wanting to be a part of it: New York, New York. Her signature red hair piled high like a skyscraper, the music all drums and big bass and her trembling vibrato.

I'd seen Tina perform this number a thousand times. The novelty of her singing live had worn off for me, but something about hearing her sing it to the dozen or so of us at Industry that night made it feel different this time. The way she was trying to be funny while her voice trembled with fear, the fact that half of us watching were employees who were about to lose our jobs. You could feel the anticipatory grief in the room, the cruel irony of listening to a song about dreaming of coming to the city while in reality thousands of New Yorkers were fleeing it.

My eyes misted over, remembering all the years I'd spent in Florida dreaming of one day making it here too. *You did it,* I thought. *You're here.* I wasn't sure whether to laugh or cry. All those years, everything I'd had to do to get to this place, and for what? They were saying the world was ending, and I was wiping down tables at some gay bar in Hell's Kitchen.

I wish I was one of those people who were able to learn a new language in the pandemic. Or who bought a sewing machine or repainted their bathroom or perfected their sourdough bread recipes. In the beginning, when I wasn't freaking out about money, I didn't do much at all except sleep and try to figure out how to apply for unemployment. This was when many of us thought quarantine might last a couple weeks at most, and government officials were sending out confusing messages about the severity of the virus, downplaying the real death count.

I was still living in the Bed-Stuy apartment that Diego had helped me move into the year before. After our breakup, he'd disappeared completely. He deleted all social media, didn't come around for the clothes he left behind. Without any closure, it had taken me longer than I would like to admit to get over him. I was heartbroken for months, yet Diego had made it seem so easy to move on, as if I never crossed his mind again after that morning at the park when he'd said it was getting too hard to consider me. I pictured him holed up in a studio somewhere, painting, while all I could do was replay every scene from our relationship, searching for a clue as to why he didn't want to be together anymore, or else bore my friends with the same old story about the one who got away. When even I couldn't take how pitiful I was becoming, I decided I had to move on too. I couldn't sit around waiting for him, drowning in endless what-could-have-beens. Besides, what good did it do to fantasize about homes with white picket fences when I could barely cover my portion of the rent on an apartment I shared with three roommates?

Priorities. I was almost thirty. Living paycheck to paycheck. One of my fake teeth was loose. The dentist who put them on had warned me they'd have to be replaced in fifteen years, which was right around the corner. I really needed to get my shit together before that happened. So after forcing myself to accept that Diego and I were done, I rerouted the energy I'd used on him into writing, the best shot I believed I had at escaping the cycle of dead-end jobs I'd become trapped in.

The year leading up to the pandemic, I spent every spare second I had finishing the book I started in grad school, writing on the train to work, on the back of receipts, on my phone between taking drink orders. In the morning I printed out chapters in the offices of the restaurant group, and at night I edited them by hand in the cramped break room at Industry, trying to focus while my co-workers ran in and out and the DJ blasted techno just outside the door.

The dream that my book would pull me out of poverty was a motivating factor, but whether or not it came true, writing itself nourished me. It reminded me there was something I was skilled at other than cleaning up customer's spills. Imagining a future reader out there who might learn from my mistakes made me feel like there was value in my failures. Imagining another reader caring about what I had to say took the sting out of the memory of when a blond twink at Industry threw his two-dollar tip at my face after I'd delivered his drink, as if I were nothing, just his servant, then turned around and continued dancing as the bills fell limply to the floor. I wanted to cuss him out and slap him. Instead, I took a deep breath, walked into the nearest bathroom, and repeated to myself: *Relax. Control yourself. You can't get fired now. You're so close. One day, you'll be a published author and he'll be begging for your autograph, okay?*

I had titled my manuscript *High-Risk Homosexual*, the diagnosis I received from a doctor a few years earlier when I signed up for the medication Truvada, the one-a-day pill that reduces your risk of contracting HIV by nearly 100 percent. At first, I'd been disturbed that my doctor printed "high-risk homosexual" on my prescription; it sounded like a relic from the times when queerness was treated with electroshock therapy. I showed my prescription to some of my friends who were on Truvada, and they all had the same thing written on theirs. Eventually it became sort of funny to me that our doctors would label us "high-risk" when in reality we were doing something not at all risky; on the contrary, we'd sought out a medication that would keep us healthy. I wanted to turn those words back on them, on any-one who ever underestimated me.

When an agent agreed to represent me and gave me notes on the manuscript, I took it as a sign that I was on the right track and buckled down harder, canceling all plans because I had to stay home writing, setting my alarm for five a.m. so I could squeeze in an hour of editing before heading off to pull another double, or work one of my other side hustles: substitute teach-ing, coat checking, dog walking. I was aware that to make a living as an artist would take sacrifices. For the rest of the year, I lived on Red Bull and dollar slices of pizza to cut down my time cooking, neglected my friendships, went months between calls to my mother. Nothing mattered to me more. In my des-peration to make it as a writer, Diego's words made perfect sense: It was too hard to consider anyone else. At the end of each night, I dropped into bed exhausted and alone, clutching my laptop like a life raft, like the stories inside would save me.

Once the book was ready in February 2020, I sent the new draft to my agent, who said she'd start pitching it to publishers. In the meantime, I went to work and counted down the days.

By the third week of lockdown, when it became clear we were in this for the long haul, I had only one person on my mind.

"Essential workers," the government was calling folks like my mother. News outlets branded them "heroes." Doctors who risked their lives to treat Covid patients. Emergency room nurses who slept in their garages to avoid infecting their families. But also the drivers delivering Amazon boxes with cough medicine to our front steps, the grocery store clerks, the pilots and flight attendants. While businesses all over the country were shuttering their doors, the airports had remained open so people could fly back home to quarantine with their loved ones, and those people liked to buy coffee before their flights, so the Starbucks at the Orlando airport where my mother had been working as a barista for two decades now had to stay open in the pandemic too.

Every day I woke up terrified she would get infected. At fifty-six, with a medical history that included a stroke and a battle with cancer, she was actually high-risk and working at one of the riskiest places around—stories of people with Covid flying in planes and spreading it to everyone on board were all over the internet. Several times a week I asked her if Starbucks had closed her location yet, why people couldn't make do without coffee for a few hours to protect employees, if she could please stay home, questions that she patiently answered with: "If I stay home, they'll fire me, then they won't give me unemployment if they let everyone go."

"Mamá, that doesn't matter," I pleaded, though of course it did. "I'll send you money."

"It's okay," she said. "I'll be fine."

She reminded me of myself, the two of us risking everything to serve drinks to tourists.

"Pero Mamá, what if something happens to you? What if . . ."

She smacked her lips through the phone. "Come on. Don't you know your mamá? When I was a little girl in Nicaragua, I was always swimming in rivers, playing in the mud, your abuelita feeding us iguana soup. Ni Covid, ni nada. I can handle it. I'm strong."

I'd heard that word before. *Strong*. It was what my aunts had told her to be before she had her stroke when I was twelve. What everyone called people who'd gone through something hard. So resilient, so tough. They said these words like they were supposed to be compliments, but I was beginning to recognize them for what they truly were: a cheap consolation prize given in exchange for our time, labor, and health. My mother did not need to be strong. She needed to stay home. Who was her strength serving? The bottom line of a company that didn't care if she lived or died? The same company that, after twenty years, still paid her only ten dollars an hour?

Despite her bravado, I knew she was scared. My mother didn't play around with getting sick. She kept an arsenal of ginger tea, VapoRú, and mysterious, unlabeled pills that relatives sent her from Nicaragua in her medicine cabinet at all times. Covid was her worst nightmare. And because her marriage with my stepdad, Omar, had been on the rocks for years, she was essentially on her own. They slept in different bedrooms, lived separate lives.

I called several times a week to distract her, racking my brain for conversation topics that weren't depressing: *The Real Housewives,* which we both watched for the low-stakes drama and gaudy fashion; my brother, who was about to have a baby in Miami and was working more than ever to save up before the due date came; musicians we'd kill to see live: Shakira, Tina Turner, her "boyfriend" Bon Jovi. I asked her what she would like to do when the pandemic was over. She said she wanted to travel the world and visit all the places her customers at the airport had told her about over the years. She was beloved at her Starbucks location, especially by the flight crew members who she hooked up with free drinks and extra shots of espresso. To show their appreciation, they promised to comp her plane tickets if she ever flew with their airlines. "One day," she always said to them, when she could take some time off. "One day," she told me now, "after the pandemic, I'm going to Spain. I want to walk El Camino de Santiago, see the cathedrals. You think it'll be cold there? Probably, right?" Mostly, she said she wanted to sleep. Fix up some things around the house that needed repairing and get her hands dirty in her garden.

After a few months, her managers finally agreed to cut her hours—not because they cared about her health but because fewer people were traveling and Starbucks had less business coming in. If I thought about it too much, the vein in my forehead throbbed, so I just focused on the relief I felt knowing she'd be slightly safer and tried helping her make up for the lost income, sending her care packages with thermometers and face masks and whatever money I could from my unemployment checks. I wanted to send more, but I didn't receive as much from unemployment as I'd been expecting: my job at Industry had been under the table and therefore ineligible for welfare benefits, so I'd had to apply based on the reduced pay I had made in the last couple of weeks at the restaurant group, when I was getting fewer shifts.

One of my roommates, Joseph, saw that I was anxious and suggested I apply for food stamps. When I discovered I could use them online, I told my mother a lie about having a ton of extra food stamp money left over so she wouldn't object to me shipping her groceries. Milk. Loaves of bread. Plus things I knew she'd enjoy but wouldn't justify purchasing for herself: good olive oil; local, grass-fed meat. She said it was too much, that the food stamps were for me, what was I eating?

I was fine. I could make a carton of eggs last a long time.

"Don't worry," I told her. "Didn't you know? I'm strong, like you."

Joseph and I had been quarantining in our apartment alone together since our two other roommates left the city in March. I'd known him for almost a decade. We'd met as college students in Orlando while working at a call center and had stayed friends after he graduated and moved back to Bed-Stuy, where he was raised. When I moved to New York, he offered to rent me a room that opened up in his apartment right as my sublease in Sunset Park ended.

Though we'd been roommates for a year already by the time the pandemic began, I'd barely gotten to see him. My life in New York before Covid had been all about hustling: first, to find a job, then to pay my bills and get an agent, and finally, to write my book. The only friends I saw regularly were my co-workers, who made me think it was normal to let your relationships wither because, like me, they were all artists busy chasing their dreams: they were dancers, actors, playwrights, drawn to the city for the opportunities they'd been told existed here.

In the bleakest, early days of the pandemic, the most I could do was lie in bed staring at the ceiling, despairing at the sound of nonstop ambulance sirens blaring through my open window. Every now and then Joseph knocked on my door to share something he'd cooked with me—steaming plates of coconut rice; mugs of sweet, cinnamony sorrel—a gesture so kind that I eventually dragged myself out of my room to keep him company. After being so focused on my personal goals, it felt like I was re-meeting my friend, this person I slept under the same roof as and yet hardly ever hung out with. Joseph and I spent hours on the living room couch in our pajamas, watching our favorite *Wendy Williams Show* clips, cracking each other up writing corny rap lyrics, telling each other our hopes for the future, how nervous we were, how nervous we'd been since long before the pandemic about the gradual stripping away of our rights.

In June, during Pride month, I confessed to Joseph that I missed Industry. It wasn't the best job, but I got to be around gay people and see drag shows, drink for free. The next day after dinner, he got up in a hurry and went to his room without saying why. A few minutes later, as I was washing the dishes, he called me over. "Edgar! Come here!"

"Hold on!" I shouted from the kitchen sink. "I'm not done."

"Just come!" he insisted.

I walked down the hallway to his room, trying to guess what this was about, when I heard the faint din of music growing louder as I approached. "What's up?" I asked through his door.

He opened it, and suddenly the hallway filled with flashing strobe lights and the sound of the new Lady Gaga album blasting out of a speaker tucked under his desk. "Welcome to Club

Rona!" he yelled, pressing a bottle of tequila into my hands. "Let's get white girl wasted, bitch!"

My eyes lit up, taking in how he'd transformed the room. He'd pushed aside all his furniture to make a dance floor for us, hung up paper stars from the ceiling. We couldn't go to a gay bar, so he'd brought one to me.

As the two of us danced and passed the bottle back and forth, our neighbors in the apartment across from ours laughing at us through their blinds, I was grateful we had each other to lean on at the end of the world.

Outside, the city had put a curfew banning anyone who wasn't an essential worker from leaving their apartments after eight p.m. It was partly a pandemic safety measure, though it was obvious to anyone paying attention that they were also trying to put an end to the protests sweeping through New York in response to Black and brown people being murdered by the police with impunity.

It had been months since I stepped out of our apartment when I attended my first pandemic protest, double-masked, the phone number to a national bail fund network written in Sharpie on my thigh in case I got arrested as I marched alongside thousands of New Yorkers carrying signs demanding justice for Breonna Taylor, George Floyd, and Layleen Polanco.

Reading the news in isolation, I'd been overwhelmed by how big the problems of the world were compared to how small I was: Police brutality. Anti–queer and trans legislation. Immigrant children being separated from their families by ICE. What could one person feasibly do to make a difference? Pandemic protests reminded me about solidarity in numbers, that it was my ego telling me that I had to solve every problem or do nothing at all. No one was asking me to solve every problem. At protests, each person served a specific role. Cyclists blocked roads from traffic. Volunteers handed out PPE and water. Legal observers recorded arrests. Organizers led chants on bullhorns. People behind them echoed those chants at the top of our lungs. It gave me hope to accept that I wasn't able to do everything. All I had to do was play my part. Still, it shamed me to think that for the last couple of years, I'd been so focused on surviving and getting a book deal that I'd neglected to do anything of use for anybody else.

All along, I had justified taking the people in my life for granted by telling myself that selling my book would give me the money to help them. I'd be able to pay off my mother's debt, buy my hungry friends lunch. I resented the professor I had in graduate school who, while discussing a book we'd read for his class, had declared with disgust that "you can always tell when the writer only cares about money." I'd wanted to tell him that I was sorry he could probably smell the poverty on my stories, sorry for sullying the purity of the art form by privately hoping it would both feed *and* fulfill me. He was likely referring to writers who make money their sole objective, often at the expense of their communities, yet in the moment it had felt like he was coming for me for being poor.

As I marched through the streets, my professor's words flooded back to me. I had, in fact, been ignoring my community, claiming that the long hours I was putting in were for everyone's benefit, like an overworked parent missing their child's soccer game and defending themselves by saying, "Can't you see I'm doing this for you!" My ambition had isolated me from the people I loved most. And maybe it was all a waste of time.

But it wasn't too late. I continued attending protests, made dates to see friends I'd lost touch with on Zoom, tried to cheer Joseph up like he did me, cooking tacos for him, fixing us pitchers of spicy margaritas. When my mother called to tell me Starbucks had finally laid her off, I was thrilled, though I knew I'd have to find a way to make some money fast. Until then, I wired her more of my unemployment. It wasn't much, but as long as we were getting by, we'd be okay.

One morning I woke up to an email from my agent. I assumed it would be like the other emails she'd sent me letting me know that yet another publisher had passed on *High-Risk Homosexual,* all of which I'd dragged to the trash bin in a grim daze, too distracted by everything else going on to summon much emotion about something I'd written what felt like a lifetime ago. But the subject of this email was full of exclamation points, and when I clicked through, she'd written in all caps that a small, independent publisher based in New York was offering me $15,000 to publish the book.

I stared at the words on my screen in shock, doing the math in my head. Fifteen thousand dollars. Before taxes and my agent's commission, spread out over two years. Fifteen thousand dollars. What I'd been working toward for years. Fifteen thousand dollars. Enough to fill my fridge a little while longer, to help my mom. I wasn't about to make it rain like a real housewife, but the money wasn't everything. My dream was coming true. I sighed, reading the email over and over. Then I closed my laptop and left my room.

Joseph was sprawled out on the couch watching TV.

"So I just got an email from my agent," I said. "Guess what?"

"What?" He looked up at me.

"Oh, it's no big deal." I inspected my nails nonchalantly, and before I could finish telling him, he shot up from the couch to grab my hands and jump up and down.

"You sold your book?" he squealed. I'd been giving him updates whenever they came in. "You sold your book! Yessss! You're an author, boo! I knew you would do it!"

We stopped jumping and hugged.

"I mean, it really isn't a big deal," I told him. "No one's gonna buy it anyway."

"Oh please." He smirked. "You better not forget me when you're famous."

When our lease was up at the end of 2020, Joseph moved into a larger place in Brooklyn that was out of my price range, and another friend invited me to live with her in Jackson Heights, Queens. Erika was an immigration attorney who had been quarantining by herself and wanted some company she could trust. Her apartment only had one bedroom, but she said I could stay in her spacious living room for $500 a month—a steal in New York. I jumped at the chance.

The times I'd visited Erika in Jackson Heights, I'd fallen in love with the neighborhood: the Mexican ladies who sold tamales out of grocery carts and told me I reminded them of their nephews, the Peruvian and Ecuadorian bakeries on every block, gay bars with unapologetically horny names like Hombres and El Trio blasting sad Juan Gabriel songs into the street. Walking through Jackson Heights, surrounded by people who looked like they could all be related to me, I felt more at home than anywhere else in the city. It was a queer, Latinx, working-class sanctuary.

Erika's living room wasn't bad, but it was awkward not having any privacy, so my second month in the apartment, we put up a wall divider to give me a sort-of room.

"Damn," I said once it was done. "I just got here, and I'm already building walls. I'm basically Trump."

"Yeah." She rolled her eyes at me. "You are *exactly* like Trump."

I was exaggerating—but in truth, I understood that I couldn't simply sweep into Jackson Heights and take up space, assuming I'd be welcomed for being queer and Latinx. I needed to actually contribute to the neighborhood and build community there, especially after the past few years I'd spent working with my head down, ignoring the people around me.

On Instagram, I learned about Love Wins, a grassroots, queer-operated food pantry that was only ten blocks from the apartment. I signed up after seeing them post a call for volunteers, fondly remembering a food pantry I'd volunteered for at my college campus when I was an undergraduate student in Orlando. My first day at Love Wins, I woke up at seven and made my way over to Friend's Tavern, the gay bar that hosted the pantry.

The volunteer coordinator, Paula, met me at the front door

wearing pink cargo pants and green Doc Martens boots, like they were going to gay war. Paula gave me and another new volunteer a tour, catching us up on the story of how Friend's Tavern, which was closed because of the pandemic, had loaned Love Wins their space to run the pantry. Friend's wasn't very big, no larger than a corner café, but the team at Love Wins made use of every inch. Cans of beans and tuna and PPE supplies covered the top of the bar, bags of rice were stacked up against the walls. Volunteers walked in and out, bringing in boxes of vegetables donated by World Central Kitchen. Paula instructed us to fill plastic bags with one of everything in preparation for the community members who were already lining up outside the door to receive a collection.

"Feel free to grab one for you too, fam," Paula said.

My job, after helping fill the bags, was to walk the line, making sure everyone had masks on and stayed six feet apart, and to talk to the Spanish-speaking community members about other resources they had access to, like community fridges. The majority of the people in line were middle-aged Latin women who could have been my mother. Some had been waiting before sunrise because Love Wins often ran out of food. One of the other volunteers, an Afro-Colombian woman named Ruth with blue mermaid braids down to her butt, walked the line with me playing music on a boom box, dancing and cracking jokes. "You have to try to make it a party," she told me. "That's what makes us different than some of these other pantries, where everyone looks so miserable. They treat them like beggars. We show them a good time here."

What she said resonated with me. I looked around and saw

a drag queen in a rainbow tutu ordering people around with a bullhorn, a trans woman in six-inch sparkly heels handing out bags at the front of the line. The pantry, they'd later tell me, was about more than food.

Many of the community members who received donations were the essential workers and heroes who made New York City what it was—the tamale ladies, the restaurant workers—yet because of their undocumented immigration status, they were ineligible for social services like food stamps. We were showing them that it was queer people, not the government, who showed up to feed Jackson Heights in its time of need. We weren't anything to be afraid of.

That morning, Love Wins handed out bags of food to over five hundred families in Jackson Heights. After the last person left, the volunteers gathered in the backyard of Friend's Tavern to debrief and get to know each other more. It was there that I met Alán, one of the newer Love Wins organizers handling administrative duties. These were the last days of fall, and he wore a cowboy hat, pink polish on his fingernails, and snakeskin boots tucked into Levi's. We exchanged Instagrams. When I got home, I had a message in my inbox waiting from him.

We made plans to meet in Central Park the next day at noon. At 12:10, Alán hadn't arrived. Fifteen minutes later there was still no sign of him. The only reason I didn't leave was because I wanted to ask him who he thought he was to his face, too cool to show up on time when *he* was the one sliding into *my* DMs. I lay on the grass, pretending to read a book and quietly seething.

When Alán finally appeared, forty-seven minutes later, he wiped the sweat from his forehead and explained that he'd just moved to New York a month before and was still learning the trains. "I'm so sorry," he said. "There was no service in the tunnel. I kept trying to text you. Next time I'll leave an hour early, I swear." He produced a joint from his pocket and extended it toward me. A gift. I hadn't smoked in a while; my dealer had fled the city too.

"Uh-huh," I said bitterly lighting up. "This doesn't mean I'm not mad."

The Met Museum had recently reopened—one of the few places where people could visit while maintaining social distance—so after getting stoned in the park, the two of us went there. Even with our masks on, Alán was easy to talk to. As we strolled by ancient Roman statues and Van Gogh paintings, my annoyance at his tardiness melted away. He told me about growing up undocumented in Vado, New Mexico, working at a dairy farm and picking chiles as a teenager, taking coding classes in his early twenties, and his current job at an organization that helped first-time home buyers apply for subsidized loans. He was a genuine cowboy. By the time we left the Met, I'd spent more time admiring him than the art. I hadn't been on a date since the pandemic began a year and a half before. His jeans were . . . snug. I was ready to pounce.

For our second date a few days later, Alán invited me to La Marcha de las Putas, a transgender sex worker rally in Jackson Heights. The rally was in response to a 1976 antiloitering law in New York that police officers had been using to arrest trans women for acts such as wearing skirts in public and standing on street corners—it was commonly referred to as the "walking while trans ban." Though the law was used against trans women of all occupations, it was specifically made to target sex work, one of the few ways undocumented trans women are able to make money in a country where other opportunities are scarce.

Some women at La Marcha de las Putas shouted that all they wanted was to work and live with dignity. "Hire me!" they yelled as we charged through busy, commercial sidewalks, passing the businesses that had rejected their job applications. Others proudly proclaimed, "These corners are my office!" Alán and I marched side by side, surrounded by hundreds of trans women and their allies, everyone decked out in sexy outfits. People in the street watched the colorful procession, taking selfies, pumping their fists in the air, running over to join.

At the end of the rally, we met up at a local restaurant with Alán's friend Lesly, the trans woman I'd seen handing out bags of food at the front of the pantry line. She wore a tight, floor-length mesh dress, with black tape X's covering her nipples underneath, and had drawn a beauty mark above her full, red lips. I felt underdressed next to her in my FEMME POWER T-shirt and denim shorts, my pockets stuffed with cough drops and tissues like someone's abuelita. We ordered a round of micheladas, and as we sipped our drinks, our conversation turned to the Mirror Cooperative, a nonprofit beauty certification program Lesly and her friend Joselyn had founded at the beginning of the pandemic to offer beauty classes to trans Latinas. The idea was that they'd use their certificates to find jobs at salons as a more stable alternative to sex work, or to supplement their incomes. They weren't anti–sex work; they simply recognized the risks that came with it and wanted to give their students a chance to earn a living doing something else.

Lesly leaned closer to me, squinting through her long, spidery lashes. "You're pretty," she said. "Do you want to model for us? We always need models."

I looked from her to Alán and back and smiled.

That was how I ended up spending every Thursday night at Alán's with Lesly, Joselyn, and the trans and nonbinary students who made up the latest Mirror cohort. Alán had been loaning the cooperative his studio apartment in Sunnyside as a space to practice the makeup skills they were learning in class, since they'd have to pass a test to receive their certificates. Like the food pantry, Mirror was funded entirely through community donations, raffles, and fundraising events. Another gap left by the government, filled in by community.

I was nervous on the train heading to my first makeup practice session. In the past, I'd had men ghost me the moment I did something they deemed as too feminine, whether that was growing my hair out or ordering a fruity cocktail. I knew Alán wasn't that way—he was opening his home to Mirror, after all—yet a lifetime of men expecting me to be their macho Latin Papi fantasy made it hard for me to believe he'd find me attractive if he saw me get made up.

I arrived at Alán's place early and was immediately greeted by the scent of sage burning. His apartment was small, but he made it work. He'd spread a towel on top of his comforter for students to lay out their brushes and makeup, arranged chairs and mirrors along the walls so everyone could have their own stations. Lesly was already there. She gave me a kiss on the cheek and began fiddling with the TV's remote, confused, before turning to Alán and thrusting it at him. "Ay, put on some music. Put on Banda MS, güey!"

Paula sat by an open window, eating chips and green salsa out of a huge bowl on their lap with their Docs kicked up on a stool. "Sup," they said, throwing up a peace sign.

An hour later the apartment was full of Mirror students, six in total, along with the volunteers Alán had recruited from Love Wins to model. The students took classes with a professional at a beauty school on Tuesdays and were eager to try out the techniques they were learning on us. I was paired with a woman who had traveled two hours from New Jersey for the practice session, leaving right after clocking out of her day job as a janitor at a corporate office building so she'd make it on time—that's how much Mirror meant to her. That week, their instructor had taught them about smoky-eye makeup. My student had me lean back in my seat as she carefully shaded in my lids, blinking back the particles of eye shadow that fell on my pupils.

"Stop fidgeting," she commanded.

"Sorry," I said meekly.

Across the room, Alán and another student were in a similar pose. He had also agreed to model. Watching him in my peripheral vision, I realized that I had nothing to be nervous about. We were both getting painted. Clearly, being "too feminine" was not going to be a problem. When the students finished with our smoky eyes, they moved on to the rest of our faces, applying foundation on our skin, bronzer on our cheeks, adding pops of color to our lips. Afterward Lesly brought out wigs to complete our looks. I chose a shiny, shoulder-length black one that matched my natural dark hair and vampy makeup.

"What do you think?" I asked Alán as I secured it in place.

He tilted his head, appraising me, then kissed me on the cheek. "I think you're beautiful."

"Shut up!" I said, blushing. "You're going to ruin my makeup!"

Once everyone left, we crammed into his tiny bathroom to shower, giggling as we scrubbed each other's backs. The pandemic and not being able to see other people had pushed our relationship into overdrive: a handful of dates in, we were already acting like a corny married couple. I didn't mind. Being corny felt nice. The radiator wasn't working, so we ran out of the shower to his bed. I fell asleep curled in his arms, comforted by the heat radiating from his body, his soft, gentle snores.

That night, something began to thaw inside me, an iciness I'd been carrying in my chest since I was a teenager. For the first time in a long time, I didn't feel cold.

My mother's pandemic experience in Florida was almost the complete opposite of mine in New York. Mask mandates were hardly enforced in the Republican-run state. Applying for unemployment was a grueling, complicated process. And as people from around the country were flocking there, lured by cheap rent and fewer pandemic restrictions, Covid cases were on the rise. Since she'd lost her job, I'd kept using my food stamps to buy her groceries and sending her whatever money I had from my advance and my own unemployment checks. I told myself that once my book was out, I could try getting a university job, or convince my publisher to hire me as an editor. I just needed us to make it a little longer, and then I'd be able to take care of her the way she deserved.

My mother told me to focus on myself, repeating her favorite line about being strong. She was only six years away from turning sixty-two, and then she'd be at the earliest age eligible to retire and receive partial Social Security, though if she postponed her retirement until sixty-seven, she could receive it in full. She waved away my questions about how she was doing with money, instead keeping me up to date on our family in Nicaragua, who she was always mailing boxes of clothes and personal hygiene products she purchased in bulk at the flea market. One of her brothers had passed away from Covid, leaving his wife behind with a newborn baby girl. "We used to get into so much trouble when we were kids," Mom said, her voice flattened by grief, "but he always protected me." Another of her brothers was on critical life support. "Send him a message on WhatsApp so he can hear your voice. Tell him you love him."

Listening to how broken she sounded, I pushed away the practical part of my brain that wanted to make sure her lights didn't go out. Conversations about money could wait; they would only stress her out more.

When I mentioned that I was volunteering at Love Wins, she told me she'd started attending a food pantry run out of a church, how she was becoming friends with the Puerto Rican and Dominican ladies in line. The avocado tree she'd planted in her backyard when we first moved to Orlando had recently birthed hundreds of fruit. She kept a few for herself and gave the rest to her neighbors and to the ladies at the pantry. "They were so happy with the avocados," she said proudly. "I'm gonna take tamarindo next, when those are ready. So they can make juice."

It was just like her to be thinking of everyone but herself.

Late one afternoon, she sent me a WhatsApp message telling me that she hadn't been feeling well, but that it wasn't a big deal. "Remember when I had to go to the hospital when you were little? And what happened to my face? It happened again. But don't worry, it's nothing." I video called her immediately, my heart racing. What did she mean, "don't worry"?

When she appeared on-screen, the whole world went silent. My mom. Her face. It was the same as when she had her stroke. The Bell's palsy. Her left eye was swollen shut, her cheeks drooped half an inch like they were melting. When she spoke, only one side of her lips moved, and her words came out with a thick lisp. I wanted to wrap my arms around her and hold her to my chest, but she was thousands of miles away. I couldn't even fly to Orlando to keep her company—if I caught Covid on the plane, I could pass it to her. I was useless.

"How is this possible?" I asked, trying to hide the panic brewing inside me.

"I have an appointment with a doctor," she said. "They're going to do some tests. I'm sorry, it's hard to talk right now, I'll let you know what they say."

"La quiero mucho, Mamá," I told her, but all I could think was that the last time she was sick, she couldn't get out of bed for months, and she had been younger then.

"I love you too," she said back.

When we hung up, I sat alone in my fake bedroom, staring at the wall, clenching and unclenching my fists and holding back tears. She was so close. Six more years. That's all she had left before she could retire and do all the things she'd been waiting her entire life for. We were going to go to Spain, tend to her garden, see her boyfriend Bon Jovi.

Later that evening, Alán came over to sit with me.

"I don't understand." I leaned my head on his shoulder. "What am I supposed to do? She's my mom. My *mom*, Alán. I can't lose her . . . not again."

"I know, baby," he said. "I know."

When I was a kid, my mother and I liked to drive through the suburbs in Orlando. It would usually be on our way home from the grocery store, the two of us in her white pickup truck, a rosary dangling from the rearview mirror. We'd cruise through the neatly manicured streets, nudging each other as we passed the random Mediterranean-style McMansions in the middle of Florida. The proud Victorians shrouded by oak trees weeping Spanish moss. Speedboats covered in plastic tarps in every driveway. Sweeping lakefront views. It was more entertaining than TV.

"Look, that one's for sale," I remember her saying to me

ALIGATOR TEARS

once, pointing to a cottage house with giant windows. Inside, a girl moved around a room with floor-to-ceiling bookcases.

I narrowed my eyes, wondering if she knew how lucky she was.

"It's okay," I said.

"Yeah." Mom looked down at me. "Just okay, right? When I win the lotto one of these days, I'll get one three times as big. And not in one of these boring neighborhoods. In Miami."

"With a pool," I added. "And a jacuzzi!"

"Of course!" She smiled and switched her voice into the snooty accent that never failed to make me laugh. "How else am I going to relax without a ja-kewwwsi, darlingggg?"

Early on, Mom taught me that if you weren't satisfied with the present, there was always the dream of "one day" to look forward to.

After her first stroke, as I rushed home from the bus stop every afternoon to make sure she was still okay, I promised myself: *One day you are going to be rich and buy her a mansion in Miami, hire her a whole team of doctors and nurses.* When I grew older and entered the workforce, after clocking in another sixty-plus-hour week across multiple minimum wage jobs, I swore: *One day this won't be for nothing. Everyone has to pay their dues. Watch, soon you'll get hired somewhere you won't have to ask permission to pee. One day this will be worth it,* I privately hoped as I gave dudes I met online massages to pay my phone bill, and ate cereal for breakfast, lunch, and dinner, all the while moving into smaller and smaller apartments with more and more roommates, my body slowly wearing down from lack of sleep and malnutrition. In the meantime, I had to show my humility, be grateful I didn't have it worse, not correct the managers who snapped their fingers at me and called me "José" and "Enrique." I couldn't get fired before I made it. I couldn't ruffle the feathers of someone who might offer me an opportunity later.

I was twelve, and twenty-four, and seventeen, and thirty. So exhausted by how much it took to just barely survive, I started to believe the voices who told me my sacrifices served a greater purpose, that what didn't kill me made me stronger. The universe would pay me back in the future for today's blood, sweat, and tears with money and stability, or by allowing me into one of those cool heavens that's chill about gay people. One day everything would be better.

Witnessing the return of Mom's illness, it finally hit me how brainwashed I'd been, how flawed was the line of thinking that hard work and humility would save me. Those things hadn't saved her. And no amount of pretending things might be different one day would change that. Suddenly, I saw the archetype of the humble poor person for what it was: a scam that justifies scarcity, that tells poor folks our suffering is for our benefit, that it will build so-called strength; a dangling carrot to keep us quiet and servile while we wait for a prize that may always be out of reach. Even the dream of "one day" has been taken from us. We can't afford to buy homes. We can't afford to go to the dentist. We must take out massive loans to go to college, only to graduate into impossible job markets. Our libraries are closing while budgets increase for the police, who imprison anyone who can't afford a place to live, or mental health resources, or fare for the train. We've been told there won't be enough Social Security left for us to retire, or safe air to breathe, and that it's all our fault for having the audacity to treat ourselves to an iced coffee to stay awake.

After the call, I wanted so badly to hide in my room, like I had at the beginning of the pandemic, sinking into my mattress in despair. I didn't, not because of some secret reserve of will-power I'd been holding on to, but because my mom needed me.

In the months that followed, my brother and I did everything we could to get her Bell's palsy treated, calling doctors, scheduling exams, battling with her insurance. Eventually she was prescribed a new medicine that restored her face back to almost normal, though her other symptoms persisted: chronic migraines, fatigue. Walking to the bathroom left her out of breath. It hurt the muscles in her cheeks to laugh. I desperately tried to make her anyway.

"Mamá, vio las locas peleando this week on *The Real House-wives?*"

"Mamá, if they give you Botox again, save some for me."

"Mamá, I know this is bad timing, but I think I'm gay."

"Ha ha," she said, unamused. "Very funny."

After endless paperwork and multiple rounds of testing to prove she was sick enough, she qualified to receive disability benefits. When she told me the news, I'd been sitting on the couch checking my email for a response to one of the dozens of job applications I'd been sending out once a week. A wave of re-lief washed over me, and yet as reassuring as it was to know she'd be taken care of, I refuse to accept that as a happy ending. Work and work until your body is no longer useful to some billion-dollar corporation and the government tosses you scraps. That can't be it. I want more for her. I want her to get the years she had stolen from her back.

One of my biggest fears as a child was that I wouldn't be ready for the rapture: the day when, out of nowhere, all the perfect, sinless people would be sucked up to the sky and the regular ones would be left behind. I'm not particularly religious anymore, but some days it feels like we're already living it. When I look around me, I don't see any perfect people; just normal, flawed human beings trying to make the best with what they have. The volunteers at Love Wins, who are up before the sun is out to feed families in the neighborhood. Lesly and the students of Mirror, who insist on a life that is dignified and beautiful. The friends who housed and fed me in the pandemic, the co-workers I shared birthdays with in break rooms. My mom, who put on a pair of giant black sunglasses and lipstick to bring fruit to the ladies at her local pantry.

It frustrates me to think that the people I love may never be rewarded with everything they deserve, but I'm comforted by the fact that they don't let the current bleakness of the world keep them from fighting to make it a better place. Every day they claim their joy, dreaming out loud with me on the phone, dancing in line outside Friend's, marching through the streets.

I don't know what happens after, when this is all over. But wherever they're going, that's where I'm trying to go too.

9

PAPI ISSUES

I know not having a dad is supposed to be a sad thing, but for most of my life, I didn't really feel like I was missing out on a lot. From what I saw in high school, looking around at my friends whose parents were still together, dads were just another body taking up space in their houses. All they did was sit on the couch all day drinking and scratching their balls, or storm around yelling about how lost "this generation" was compared to when they were growing up: the boys dressing like girls, no one wanting to work anymore, blah blah blah.

And compared to *my* father, those dads were amazing! My mom never talked shit about Papi to my brother or me, I assume because she didn't want to get in the way of us having a relationship one day, but she also didn't need to. Papi's actions spoke for themselves. He was an addict who spent the years following their divorce bouncing between Florida and New York and Puerto Rico, chasing after his next high, in and out of jail and homelessness. The last time we were together was when I was thirteen, during the trip Mom sent Hector and me on to PR, where Papi was living with his adoptive mother, Titi Sixta. He spent the whole time sleeping.

If I felt anything about not having a dad, it was anger that mine could walk away from the responsibility of taking care of us so easily, leaving Mom to pick up his slack. Nobody explained Papi's addiction to me as a kid, so his abandonment had seemed like a deliberate choice. Perhaps that was unfair, but it's not as if he was around to tell me his side of the story. He didn't call, write, or pay child support. As the years passed without him sending as much as a birthday card, the few good memories we had together faded away. More pressing in my mind were the consequences that his deserting us had on our family. The constant moving around in search of stable housing, the stacks of unpaid bills on the kitchen table. I blamed him for forcing Mom to work herself sick to keep Hector and me fed, for the stress that led to her stroke. Whenever someone asked me which of my parents I looked like more, I responded loyally: *My mom.* She was the one who nearly died trying to raise me, the only parent I claimed at all.

My anger was equal parts a reaction to the dire financial state Papi left us in as it was a tether to him; my father was gone, but at least there was this feeling to connect us. Throughout my twenties, I tended to my anger like a flame, practicing elaborate speeches in the shower of what I'd say if I ever ran into him (all of them starting with a slow, delicious *You bitch . . .*). Every few months I scoured Facebook and Instagram, curious to see if he had another family now and was taking care of *them,* though I didn't have luck finding a profile, probably because he didn't own a computer. At one point, I became obsessed with a website that posted mug shots of people arrested in Florida and spent countless nights searching for him there on the chance he'd returned to the States without telling anyone. Eventually, I gave up. I had a limited amount of time. Wasting it on him felt like a betrayal when I already had a great parent in my mom.

I thought Hector and I were on the same page. Papi was basically a sperm donor. We were better off not having him in our lives. But then, two years into the pandemic, my brother called to tell me Papi had contacted him and they'd started talking again. The news confused me, and yet deep down, a part of me understood. All those nights I'd spent looking for him, trying to maintain a connection between us. I guess I'm not as tough as I like to pretend to be, because fifteen years after the last time we saw each other, I boarded a plane to Puerto Rico.

"This feels so weird," I told Hector. We were in our rental Jeep, driving from our hotel in San Juan to Ceiba, a seaside town on the eastern end of the island. The pothole-ridden road had taken us from the urban sprawl of the capital to long stretches of coast with only palm trees and wild chickens roaming in the grass fields on either side of us. "It's been so long."

"Yeah," Hector replied.

My brother was never one to say much, which is why I'd been caught off guard when he told me he'd been talking to Papi. Hector didn't tell me a lot about their conversations, just that he'd scolded our father for deserting our family. And that Papi was living in Vieques, a smaller island off the coast of mainland PR. Papi must have said the correct things, because Hector asked if I wanted to see him. Any other time I'd have said no, but the pandemic had forced me to reevaluate our relationship, reminded me of the difference between not having a dad and having a shitty one I could still try to love. Now we were driving to Ceiba to pick him up at the ferry that brought Vieques residents back and forth to the big island.

"I wonder what he looks like," I said. "You know, I used to look him up on that Florida mug shots website to see if he'd show up."

"No shit?" said Hector, scratching his patchy beard, his eyes concealed behind black Ray-Bans. "You found him?"

"Nah. There were like a million people with the last name Gomez."

"I bet." My brother smirked.

I turned on the radio to a salsa station, and within minutes, the two of us were lost in our own private thoughts. I couldn't believe we were going to be with our father soon, something I'd long ago given up thinking would ever happen. Even more surprising to me than Papi reaching out was how pleased Mom sounded on the phone when I told her. "That's great," she actually said. I figured she'd at least be a little bitter. I mean, this was the man who had left her alone with two kids and a mountain of debts that haunted her for decades.

After the call, I wasn't sure what to think anymore. I'd been angry at Papi not just for my sake but for what he'd done to her, but if she'd forgiven him, didn't I need to, too? I stuck my head out the window, closing my eyes against the warm breeze. And what if I couldn't? What if I didn't want to? What was I supposed to do with all my anger, just magically let it go?

At half past noon, a sign at the entrance to Ceiba welcomed us to the town. Fried fish and beer kiosks greeted incoming traffic. Women in aprons sat at plastic tables fanning themselves and watching videos on their phones, occasionally glancing up at passing cars.

As we pulled down the skinny road that my GPS said led to the ferry, my heart suddenly began to race. Papi would be at the other end, and I still didn't know how I felt about him. My emotions were a mix of skepticism and resentment and dread. And yet despite that, I'd spent all morning trying to figure out what to wear, eventually settling on a boring pair of khaki shorts and a gray tank top that I hoped would conceal the ember of excitement burning in my belly. After fifteen years of wondering what I'd say, finally I was going to get the chance to confront him face-to-face. I couldn't imagine us clinking glasses around the Christmas table anytime soon, but I was willing to hear him out, for Mom.

The ferry station loomed in the horizon ahead of us, the ocean beyond it glimmering under the fierce afternoon sun. We slowed down when we reached the entrance gate guarded by a pair of officers. Outside my window, I could see a couple dozen people standing under a canopy, waiting to be picked up. I leaned in closer to the glass, searching through the faces in the crowd as Hector dialed Papi's number. A man at a picnic table dug into his pockets for his phone, then looked up at us and squinted, like he was also trying to recognize Hector and me.

I took a deep breath. There he was.

Papi wore a baggy Puerto Rico flag T-shirt, a backward baseball cap with a Puerto Rico flag patch, and a small drawstring book-bag with the Puerto Rico flag printed all over it slung over his shoulder. I couldn't help grinning as I watched him get up and walk to the Jeep, picturing the closet full of clothes with Puerto Rico flags I had in my own closet. *Why are our people like this?* I thought, then quickly wiped the grin from my face and stepped out of the car.

"Ruben!" Papi called out to me, using my middle name like all my family members did. "Wow, I can't believe it! You're really here!"

"Yeahhh, how are you?" I asked, like an idiot.

I wasn't sure what the proper protocol was for meeting your long-lost dad. We gave each other an awkward hug. In my child-hood memories, Papi had been a giant, looming over life itself, but as I held him then, I realized I could touch the top of his head with my chin. I liked that. Being a bigger person than him. Papi and Hector hugged too, then we all climbed into the Jeep and took off, Hector driving, me in the passenger seat, Papi tak-ing over the back.

"Look at me with my boys," Papi laughed to himself. "All of us on my island. Acho, man, how lucky am I?"

I stared straight ahead, pretending to admire the lush greenery all around us while secretly observing him in the rearview mirror. Papi smiled, a wide gap between his two front teeth. His eyes darted from my brother to me like an eager puppy.

He clasped a hand on Hector's shoulder. "Go back up this road where you came from. I wanna make a stop at B*Well. There's one close by."

I shot Hector a look. B*Well was one of the popular weed dispensaries in Puerto Rico. Of course Papi would be a stoner. Of course that would be the first place he'd want to go.

I knew, from a Google search I'd done when I'd briefly considered staying at his house during the trip, that there were no dispensaries in Vieques. No hospital either. In fact, from 1941 to 2003, much of the land in Vieques had been occupied by the U.S. Navy. Though currently home to almost ten thousand Puerto Ricans, for decades the navy had been using Vieques as a testing site for war explosives, many of which contained napalm, uranium, and other toxic chemicals, resulting in a 25 percent higher cancer rate among Vieques residents than among those in mainland PR. The lack of a hospital wasn't a mistake, rather one of the many ways the United States has wrought havoc on Puerto Rico over the years, whether through occupation and displacement, the forced sterilization of Puerto Rican women in the 1950s and '60s, even going as far as once banning Puerto Ricans from waving the flag: the reason our people are "like this."

While it felt odd that Papi was already asking us to do him a favor, I was also relieved that we were going to pick up some weed before our day together. I was nervous as hell. Slightly overwhelmed. Smoking would give me something to do with my hands other than bite my nails.

When we made it the dispensary, Papi got out of the Jeep and told Hector and me to wait in the car, since we didn't have medical marijuana licenses and wouldn't be allowed in. The second he closed the door, I turned to Hector, trying to read the expression on his face. But my brother didn't seem impacted by the sight of our dad at all. Maybe it was because he'd been speaking to Papi for months now. This wasn't their first big interaction, like it was mine.

"He's shorter than I thought," I said.

"Man's always been short," Hector replied flatly. He nodded up and down, his forehead creased with lines like old scars.

I fiddled with my seatbelt, wishing I hadn't said anything.

"He looks okay though, right?" Hector asked after a few seconds. "Better than before?"

There was a hopeful yearning to the question that I rarely heard in my brother. We were only three years apart, but it was a significant gap when it came to Papi. I'd been in elementary school when the divorce happened, so Hector had a clearer memory of what our dad was like during those rough years. A few weeks before this trip, he'd reminded me of one of the few times when Papi had flown to Orlando to visit us. Mom had dropped us off at Burger King close to the house where she'd arranged to hand us over. Papi had shown up with painful-looking scabs all over his arms and face, smelling like he hadn't bathed. He didn't have any money and had to ask Hector, a teenager, if he could lend him some for food.

I didn't remember any of that. Mom and Hector had always

protected me from seeing Papi at his worst, and now they were ready to make peace with him, and all I could focus on was the worst. Sometimes I wondered if Papi disappearing had been for our own good—*his* way of protecting us from himself. But even if that was true, it was Mom and Hector who I felt indebted to. They were the ones I knew. Papi was a stranger.

Hector waited for me to answer. Did our dad look better? Not really. He sort of looked like someone left him out in the rain. But I could tell there was an answer my brother wanted.

"Yeah," I said, "he does."

A couple minutes later Papi came out of the dispensary, cradling a brown paper bag in his hands. He climbed back into the car and tucked it between his legs. To people outside, Hector and I could have passed for his parents, driving our son to school with his lunch.

"And now?" Hector turned on the ignition.

"You wanna go see one of your tíos?" Papi asked. "You knew him when you were kids. He lived in Titi Sixta's house with me when you visited. Remember?"

I tried to find a memory in my brain of this uncle, but nothing came up.

"Yes, Tío Mario," Hector said for the both of us. "Bald dude? Tall?"

"That's the one!"

"All right." Hector shifted the car into drive. "Let's go."

As we pulled out of the B*Well parking lot, Papi turned the paper bag upside down onto the empty seat beside him. Out fell a lighter, blunt papers, and a couple of pill bottles. Hector steered us onto the highway, following the road markers to Humacao, a half hour south of Ceiba.

"What'd you get?" I asked, looking over my shoulder.

"The cheapest sativa," Papi said. "That's all I smoke."

He bit open the plastic wrapper holding the blunt papers and unrolled one leathery sheet onto his lap, then popped the lid off one of the pill bottles, releasing the tangy, earthy aroma of weed into the Jeep. I watched him grab a pinch and arrange it neatly down the middle of the paper.

"Me too," I said. "Indica just makes me sleepy and hungry." I could already hear Alán's voice in my ear when I'd rehash the afternoon to him later. *Now I know who you got it from, my little stoner.* He'd be right. Looking back at my life, and all the times I'd turned to weed and alcohol as a coping mechanism to deal with stress or grief or simple boredom, it was clear to me that aside from my curls, I'd also inherited Papi's predisposition for addiction. I had to constantly check myself to make sure I didn't let my substance use get out of hand.

"Exactly. This is the only thing I do," Papi said as he finished rolling the blunt and sealed the paper with his tongue. "I don't even touch liquor anymore. Just weed."

As an adult, I was able to understand that it wasn't as simple as Papi being a "good" person or a "bad" one for "choosing" drugs over us, like I'd believed as a child. Rather, in those years when he'd been at the height of his addiction, he'd been suffering from a disease, to say nothing of the trauma: the trauma of being abandoned as a kid by his parents, who were also addicts. Putting his addiction into context allowed me to recognize him as a fellow human being who was doing his best to survive within larger systems of oppression. But still, my logic and reason could only go so far before I thought of my mom, who had no one to help her cope with her own illnesses because of him. What about her pain? Pain that he directly contributed to. I was tired of this endless cycle of misery. At what point would everyone in my family stop passing their trauma back and forth to one another like a game of hot potato?

Papi held the blunt over my shoulder. "Wanna get us started?" he asked.

"Okay," I said.

I lit the blunt and relaxed into my seat as the smoke traveled down my lungs, gradually making the miles and miles of plantain fields outside lusher, the sky wider and limitless.

"This is a nice car," Papi said after a while. "You need a Jeep to get around here, with all the holes in the roads."

"I used to have one like this," said Hector, tapping the steering wheel affectionately, and soon the two of them were talking about boy stuff: cars, girlfriends, Hector's time working construction, Papi's current job as a handyman in Vieques. I sat there, quietly getting high and feeling out of place and self-conscious, like I always did around straight men. I found it strange how casual they sounded having a conversation, as if they'd been apart for only a weekend, and stranger that the most Papi had said about the fifteen years since I'd last seen him was "Wow, you're really here." I'd imagined there'd be tears, a dramatic reunion. Something. But maybe he was like Hector. Not one to share his emotions. Maybe that was something *he* inherited from Papi.

As the two of them talked, Papi rolled another blunt, and another, passing them over my shoulder for me to light. I kept accepting, both because I wanted to chill and because the weak "thanks" I said as he handed me each blunt was the only thing grounding me in the Jeep. Mostly I stared out the window, brooding and picking at my nail polish. By the time we made it to Humacao, I was uncomfortably high. Paranoid I wasn't speaking enough. I sank lower into my seat, intimidated by the idea of making small talk with an uncle I hadn't seen in over a decade. I'm sure he was cool, but at the moment, I could barely handle meeting my father.

We drove down the sleepy village nestled at the foot of a mountain where Tío Mario lived, passing several abandoned-looking houses with shattered windows and missing doors, before rolling to a stop in front of Tío's place. Dwarf palm trees and potted plants crowded the yard. Papi dialed Tío's number, to no response. Papi dialed again, then got out of the car and yelled, "Mariooo!" through the rusty iron gate. After a few minutes, he climbed back into the car and shrugged. "Must be out," he said. "Let's go to the cemetery, since we're already here."

I sighed, relieved.

Hector turned the Jeep around, and Papi guided us toward a smaller mountain not far off. We drove up a series of narrow, winding roads bordered by dense foliage, branches slapping against the sides of the car as we sped by. The cemetery was about halfway up the mountain and sat on a flat piece of land overlooking the scattered country homes below.

Once we parked in the gravel lot, Papi climbed out and led

the way through the crumbling archway. "Diablo, it's been a minute since I been back," he said as he walked ahead of us around shallow puddles of rainwater, pausing every few seconds to read the names on graves, all of them built above ground to protect the bodies buried inside from the frequent floods in the area. Finally, Papi found one he knew: an uncle or a cousin. He placed a hand on the headstone and looked to my brother and me. I smiled, preparing for him to open up to us.

Papi chuckled to himself. "This man," he said, voice filling with nostalgia, "he was a real piece of shit. A real son of a bitch, let me tell you. Used to beat the shit out of his kids."

My jaw dropped. I side-eyed Hector, who shook his head like *Bro, this is dad. What'd you expect?*

Papi took us to another grave. "And this one!" he said. "He hit your titi once. You know that woman raised me, she was like my mother. I came home one day and found her with a black eye. This fucker—who hits an old woman? He said it was an accident. God saved his life that day, I don't know how I didn't kill him. The police had to come tear us apart."

Papi showed us a couple more graves, telling Hector and me who was an alcoholic thief, which one had hungry children in every town from there to Miami, and which one was a greedy bastard and only cared about securing an inheritance. He reminded me of myself, every time a friend had asked me about my father over the years and I'd rolled my eyes and said *Who?* I didn't want to be the kind of person who carried a grudge all the way to the end. He never hit Mom, never abused us. His biggest crime had been neglect. It shamed me that I was unable to forgive Papi for something as capitalistic as not paying child support. Now that I was older, financially stable, and didn't depend on his money anymore, how was it serving me to be petty?

"I was messed up back then," Papi told us as we walked back to the car. "It wasn't easy. I never hid my problems from you two. There were days I didn't have anywhere to sleep. That's why I had to go to Vieques, to get away from temptation and the crazy people I was hanging out with. One of your aunts lent me a place to stay, and I been there ever since."

I let his words sink in, wondering how I would have explained who he was to my own kids if we hadn't reunited and I'd visited his grave decades later. *This is your abuelo. He left when I was little. He was . . . short. Sorry, that's all I got.*

Back in the passenger seat, I watched him strap his seatbelt on in the rearview mirror. It didn't have to end that way, I thought. Papi wasn't dead. We still had time to add to our story.

We were driving down the hill again when the scent of fried plantains from a nearby kiosk wafted into the car. Hector pulled over so we could grab alcapurrias and something to drink, then the three of us took our food to a picnic table, where we washed our greasy food down with bottles of water. A stray cat emerged from beneath a parked car and strolled up to our table, purring.

Papi asked how Mom was doing. Apparently, Hector had told him about her Bell's palsy.

"She's okay," I said. "It was scary for a minute, but her doctors are helping her. There's better treatments now. She's tired and can't do much, but she's looking like herself again."

"That's good," Papi said. "That woman is tough."

I bit my tongue, wanting to say: *Tough because she had to be.*

"Yeah," I said. "She's been through a lot." I took another sip of my beer and tore off a piece of my alcapurria, dropping it by my feet, where the cat promptly pounced on it.

"We come from a long line of tough women," Papi said. "I was sad when I found out your abuela died. How long has it been, five years? That one got to me. I remember after you were born, your mom cried and cried and begged me to send for her from Nicaragua. That lady was like fifty already and crossed the Rio Grande on foot to come take care of you."

I'd heard the story a million times before: Abuela crossing the U.S. border illegally. She wasn't about to let some paperwork get in the way of her seeing her grandbabies.

"She used to carry a knife in her purse," I said, grinning. The image of her rushed back to me. Her gray hair, powdery perfume. "After she got robbed on the bus in Nica. It was like a prison weapon. She'd wrapped a piece of broken glass with tape so she could hold it."

Papi laughed. "Oh yeah," he said. "That sounds like your abuela. You didn't wanna mess with her. Cussed me out a few times, but I deserved it. She had a big heart."

"What about your mom?" I asked. "What was she like?"

"She wasn't around a lot. Before Titi Sixta, my abuela raised me."

He told us about his grandmother, a Black woman who'd fostered in him an early love for cooking. Pasteles. Habichuelas. Her sazón, unmatched in their neighborhood. He told us about being a teenager on the island, camping out at the Yunque rainforest, the night he and his siblings had gotten drunk and tried to knock down the statue of Christopher Columbus in Viejo San Juan. As he spoke, my imagination lit up, Papi's side of my family tree sprouting branches. I wanted to hear more about my great-grandmother, about Titi Sixta too, and all the tough women I came from. But I was getting ahead of myself. I needed to know *him* before I could know them.

When Hector called to tell me he'd gotten back in touch with Papi, my first instinct had been to ask myself why. Wasn't every minute we spent on this man a minute less that we'd get to be with the people who had been there for us, like Mom? Not only that, but it would be expensive to visit, taking away money I could send to her. I hated how transactional my response was to what should've been happy news. This wasn't a business relationship. He was my father. But after all the effort I'd put in to create a life for myself without him, I needed reassurance that if I was going to welcome him back in, he'd add something to it, not just take.

The more time I spent with Papi, however, the more I understood that he did actually have something to offer that would make opening up the old wound he left me with worthwhile, things I valued more than money, like a connection to my past, to my relatives, and to this island that held so many of my family's stories.

I realized I had a choice.

I could keep him at a distance, blaming him as the root of all my money problems.

Or I could try to meet Papi where he was and give him a

second chance. All my life, I'd heard how politicians attempt to stoke the country's anger by blaming the people I love for our poverty, painting us as lazy and welfare queens, refusing to acknowledge the institutional racism that permeates everything from the school system to healthcare and the workforce, the infinite ways people in power have found to protect their wealth. It's easier to say my father was a deadbeat dad than address how gentrification, domestic violence, lack of mental health resources, and food and housing insecurity put people in desperate situations. Was I all that different than those politicians, directing my anger at Papi instead of putting it to good use by fighting for a universal basic income and support and care for drug users? Losing my father had already cost me so much; was I also willing to lose my compassion? My empathy?

Whatever the future held for us, it'd been fifteen years since Papi walked away from our family. I loved him—I do—but we wouldn't find our way back to each other overnight.

The sun had dipped below the clouds by the time we merged onto the highway again, our bellies full. Papi suggested we go to Playa Siete Mares, a beach in Fajardo where we could catch the sunset. Our day would be over soon, then we'd have to drop him off at the ferry.

He rolled another blunt as Hector drove, and the three of us cruised down the road, an old-school reggaeton station on the radio drowning out the silence. We listened to Tego Calderón and Ivy Queen, passing the blunt back and forth. It must have been our fifth or sixth of the day. The amount Papi smoked was kind of wild to me. I wanted to ask if this was normal for him, but as I racked my brain for a way to phrase my question that wouldn't be rude, it occurred to me that he was probably nervous too. There had to have been a thousand unsaid things bouncing around both our heads, but for now, being together again, listening to the radio, was enough.

We found a spot in the parking lot and took off our shoes before getting out of the car, walking barefoot along the asphalt toward the beach. It was mostly empty except for a family grilling burger patties under a palm tree, the sound of their cozy laughter drifting in the breeze.

When we reached the shore, I dipped my toes into the water. "How is it?" Hector asked.

"It feels nice," I told him. "Warm."

"Cool," my brother said. He stripped off his T-shirt and jeans until he was down to his tighty-whities, then ran into the water like a kid. Hector was always more impulsive than me. It was my favorite thing about him. After all, if he hadn't answered Papi's call, I wouldn't have been here.

Papi and I stayed behind on the shore, watching Hector crash into waves, sink below, claw himself back up before doing it again and again. "Y'all coming?" he screamed.

"Should we?" Papi turned to me.

I picked up Hector's clothes and dropped them a few feet back in the sand, where the rising tide couldn't get them.

"I don't know," I said. "It's about to be night. I don't want to be wet after dark. It'll take forever to get dry, and I can't stand the cold. I'm a baby."

"I can't either," Papi said. "I'm just going to go in up to my ankles."

He didn't ask me to go with him, but he stood there, waiting, the sky behind him streaked pink and gold. In the distance, Hector swam toward the horizon, his body silhouetted against the setting sun. It looked fun, even if it might not be worth it later. I didn't want to miss out.

"All right," I told him. "I'll go in, but just up to my ankles too."

"Just our ankles," Papi said, smiling, and the two of us took a small step forward.

10

EVERYTHING WE
EVER WANTED

Two weeks before my book was set to be published, I made my way through the crowded sidewalks of Long Island City, the bougier side of Queens, feeling self-conscious in my T.J.Maxx winter boots among the hordes of affluent New Yorkers around me. I was only a fifteen-minute train ride from Jackson Heights, but passing artisanal cheese shops and shiny microbreweries lit up with Christmas lights, I might as well have been in a different world, one where even the dogs were a little dead in the eyes. I picked up my pace, longing to get back to my own world where the air was warm with the steam from street food vendors and I couldn't go a block without someone calling me amor or trying to sell me a Social Security card. The address I'd typed into my phone's GPS led me to a sleek, silver residential high-rise. I stepped through the building's front doors and texted the number a friend had given me: *I think I'm here?*

A few minutes later my phone buzzed: *Hope you found the place easy enough. Just tell one of the attendants you're here to see me and they'll call you an elevator!*

Everything was happening faster than I could have ever imagined. It seemed like just yesterday that my agent had emailed with the news that she'd sold my book. In the rush of completing edits, volunteering at Love Wins and Mirror, and visiting Papi, I'd barely had a moment to stop and think about what I'd done or to plan anything to celebrate. I hated asking people for help, but I'd hesitantly agreed when one of the organizers of Love Wins insisted on planning a book launch party for me at Friend's Tavern, the gay bar that hosted the pantry.

Over drinks one night, my friend Mark had asked me what I would wear to the launch party if I could choose anything at all, no limitations.

"J.Lo's Versace dress," I said without hesitating. The sheer, floor-length gown with a green tropical leaf pattern that she'd made famous while presenting at the 2000 Grammys lived in my head rent-free. It was chic, slutty, and perfectly matched the palm leaf cover my publisher had designed for the book.

Mark laughed. "You're kidding," he told me.

"Damn, okay," I said, slightly offended. "You don't think it'd look good on me?"

He shook his head. "No, no, sorry, I mean that I have a friend who does costume design and dressed up as her in that dress for Halloween last year! I can ask him to lend it to you."

It was a tale as old as time: every gay person knows another gay person who knows a gay person who has a spare knockoff J.Lo Versace dress lying around. A few days later Mark texted me that I just had to pick it up and gave me the address to his friend's place. That was the reason I'd ventured out of my Jackson Heights bubble to go to Long Island City.

Ceazar greeted me at the door to his pristine twentieth-floor apartment and whisked me into his at-home studio, where he had the dress on display on a mannequin. My eyes widened in disbelief as I ran my fingers down the soft, translucent fabric. It was magical. It even *smelled* like J.Lo, like good lotion and yacht money. "It's beautiful," I said. Then I looked from the mannequin to Ceazar and back, a lump forming in my throat. He had to have been at least twenty pounds lighter than me, a fitness gay with six-pack abs and a tight gym booty.

"This is just a fitting," he reassured me as I tried to squeeze my ass into the tiny green panties he'd made since the dress was see-through. "I'll adjust it for you."

"You don't have to do that," I said, sucking my stomach in and holding my breath to get the rest of the dress on. "You're so nice for letting me wear this."

"Not a big deal at all. It's my pleasure."

I would have hugged him, but I was afraid the seams would burst if I moved my arms. Ceazar circled me, wrapping measuring tape around my chest and waist and sticking pins into the fabric. "So Mark told me you wrote a book." He smiled. "That's exciting. How does it feel?"

Being next-to-naked in front of him lured me into a false sense of intimacy. He'd been so generous with me; the bare minimum I could offer was conversation. "I don't know," I started to say. "It's . . ." I paused for a second, not sure how much to tell him. Then I remembered I was speaking to a stranger. "It's cool." I smiled back. "Honestly, I'm still in shock."

"Well, I hope you're proud of yourself," he said, so earnestly it hurt.

"Thanks," I told him. "Seriously. This dress is going to make the whole party."

An hour or so later, I walked out of Ceazar's apartment building, relieved to have one aspect of my book launch preparations out of the way. Yet as I boarded the train home, his question echoed in my ears. How did it feel? It should have been an easy answer. In two weeks, I would be a published author. Folded over my lap was the perfect dress, tailored to my exact measurements. There was nothing more I could possibly ask for. My dreams were coming true.

I stared out the train window, watching the faces of people waiting on platforms blur as we passed by.

So why couldn't I just say I was happy?

When I started my creative writing graduate school program in 2016, I had a fair amount of hope that I'd publish a book one day. Like many other MFA students, I'd studied writing at the undergraduate level and had been an avid reader my entire life, since I was a kid in Florida, bouncing between relatives' houses and low-income apartments, turning to literature to discover what else was out there. Books transported me to Russia, Egypt, Japan, allowed me to taste foods I'd never heard of and get to know how other people lived. It didn't occur to me that I could write about myself until I took my first creative writing class in college, when a professor asked me to turn in a personal essay, and I became obsessed with writing about *my* foods, *my* surroundings, *my* people, with making *us* the main characters. To be the main character was to matter. It was self-preservation in a world that seeks to erase our existences.

I had followed that obsession to graduate school in California, buoyed by the positive feedback I'd gotten on stories in the past, and slightly naïve about how publishing worked. It didn't take long for me to get a reality check. I quickly learned that the industry is dominated by wealthy people who have the spare time to write and prior connections, that only 16 percent of all books published in the United States were by LGBTQIA+ authors, and just 6 percent by Latin ones, leaving me guessing how many intersected with both, and that those few of us lucky to make it then had to contend with book bans and rising censorship across the country. Which is to say that by the end of my first year, I was well aware that it'd take a miracle for me to become an author.

Still, I had fun writing my little stories, the program gave me work and health insurance as a teaching assistant, and the alternative was going back to the Flip Flop Shop in Orlando, so I stayed, figuring I had nothing to lose. For the next two years I had left, I sat in my classes and enjoyed getting to be a student, dreading the day it'd end and I would barely have a minute to read again, much less talk for hours about writing. One of my favorite recurring subjects that came up in the program was how difficult it was to write about the people in our lives. "If someone doesn't want me to write about the bad things they did to me, they shouldn't have done them," a classmate of mine argued. Another insisted she always found something good to say, no matter who it was. Everyone had an opinion: Conceal identities. Ask permission first. Ask yourself, *Is the story I'm writing worth sacrificing the relationship?*

As compelled as I was hearing about their ethical considerations, they were irrelevant to me, because the odds were that my memoir about coming of age as a nonbinary Latinx person would never make it into a bookstore anyway. Strangely though, instead of encouraging me to give up, that realization liberated me. When it was my turn to write stories for class, I felt free to tell the truth without being paralyzed by the fear of how my family would react to me putting our business out there.

Years later, when my agent told me the news that my book sold, I couldn't stop laughing and thinking, *Holy shit! You did it! You did it! You beat THE ODDS, bitch! You did WHAT THEY SAID YOU COULDN'T DO.* Briefly, I wondered whether teenage me would have been brave enough to carry a book that had *High-Risk Homosexual* in giant letters on the cover. There were a few months when I'd considered changing the title because of a piece of advice I'd been given to try to make it more "universal." I was glad I hadn't. I owed that to my younger self.

My celebrating didn't last long, however, because when I eventually sat down to begin my final edits, all the concerns that my classmates had warned about in grad school came crashing down on me at once. I hadn't made anyone in my family look like a villain, but I was honest about how they'd responded to my queerness, both their initial rejection of me and their slow, painful journey to acceptance.

With my contract signed, it was too late to ask whether what I'd written was worth sacrificing my relationships. Even if I had asked, there was this added catch-22: writing our story is what helped me understand why my family behaved the way they did and laid the foundation for us to rebuild our relationships; now publishing it might tear us apart again.

I stared at the manuscript on my laptop, the manuscript that had made it possible for me to feed my mother and me throughout the pandemic, the manuscript that I'd prayed would set us up to have better lives, and all I could think was: *If she finds out about this, it'll ruin everything.*

More than anyone else in my family, it broke my heart that I couldn't tell her. As much as I wanted to be a writer, she wanted that for me more. After graduating from the program, my mother made sure to message me on WhatsApp every few months encouraging me to keep going. *You're the artist of the family,* she'd say. *What are you working on?* And *Saw a commercial today about a company that publishes books. Let me find out their name.*

Each time I played coy, changing the subject.

Ever since the day I came out to my mom and I heard her crying on the phone with an aunt, I'd put up a boundary between us to hide the queer parts of my life from her. I didn't like talking to her about boyfriends, whatever was going on with my gender, or anything that might make her love me less, regardless of how much she'd come around in the years since then. But the truth is I always had an excuse to keep my writing a secret from my mom: When I first moved to New York, it was *This probably won't go anywhere anyway.* When her brother passed away in the pandemic, it was *You can't tell her while she's grieving.* When her Bell's palsy returned, it was *You have to wait until she's healthier. It could make her sicker.*

Now, as the publication date approached, the idea of telling her felt more daunting than ever. Surely she would be upset that I'd waited so long, and she would be right to be.

At home in Jackson Heights, I sighed and hung the Versace dress in a corner of my closet. Ceazar had done an amazing job. It really was beautiful. More beautiful than I deserved.

The day of the book launch, I woke up in bed next to Alán, our legs tangled together, the radiator hissing hot air into the small room we'd been sharing since he moved in with me and Erika a few weeks earlier. I pulled my arm from beneath his snoring body and kissed him on the forehead, then quietly padded out to the kitchen to make us coffee.

In the months leading up to pub day, I'd been paranoid that something would happen to me before the book was released. An AC unit would fall on my head while walking down the sidewalk, or I'd trip and fall onto the train tracks. Something was bound to go wrong. I didn't trust how, out of nowhere, my life had reversed course. I was the person who got expelled from high school, who mopped up lube at the sex club, and somehow I'd stumbled into this alternate universe where I was also the person who lived with his boyfriend in New York (albeit in a fake room), had a book soon-to-be out, and an inbox full of journalists asking me about my "process."

I carried my coffee to the living room couch, the caffeine slowly waking me up as I took inventory of this life I had difficulty believing was actually mine. The apartment was a mess of Alán's moving boxes and stuff that the women of Mirror kept around since we'd started hosting their beauty classes at our place: lighting equipment and hairbrushes and makeup. There were specks of glitter embedded in the carpet. Someone had left their ratty blond wig on top of a floor lamp. From the coffee table, I grabbed a copy of my book, opened it, and pressed my nose inside, inhaling the woodsy scent of paper and dust. It smelled like . . . a book. Like a real book.

I skimmed through some of the chapters, trying to figure out what section to read at the party at Friend's Tavern later that night. As I flipped through the pages, it struck me how many of them were saturated with a sense of fear and impending doom: that by embracing my queerness, my family would disown me or I'd die from a hate crime, that my life would be a tragic cautionary tale. Looking around at my life now, however, I understood how lucky I was—that in fact, it was a *privilege* to be gay. Had I been born straight, I probably would have gotten a girl knocked up in high school and stayed in Florida, stuck at a job I hated to support my children, or maybe I'd have joined the army like so many of the boys I graduated high school with. It was because of my queerness that I was able to see how the paths set out for me weren't enough, pushing me to leave home in search of more. Since then I'd gotten to live all over the country. To take my time discovering what I was passionate about. When I wasn't confident in myself or my choices, I always felt secure in knowing I could count on a built-in community wherever I went: a pantry to feed me, friends who'd offer me housing, work, or a dress to borrow. Being gay allowed me to not settle until I had the life I'd dreamed of as a kid.

I closed the book and sat with it for a long moment while Alán woke up, put on his cowboy hat, and groggily went out to fetch breakfast from the tamale lady down the block. As I finished my coffee and my phone blew up with "Happy pub day!" texts, I wondered what my mom would think if she knew how far I'd come. How far *we'd* come. After all, this accomplishment wasn't mine alone. She was my main character, the person who mattered to me most.

Eventually Alán returned with our tamales and a bouquet of pink roses from the deli. He ran around the apartment looking for a vase, but the two we had were already full with flowers that had arrived from friends while he'd been out. He told me to hold on and went into the kitchen, then came out again seconds later with his bouquet soaking in a blender.

"Really?" I asked, raising an eyebrow.

He reminded me of a telenovela star, all square jaw and pretty brown eyes. "Come on! What was I supposed to do?" He grinned and set the blender on the coffee table with the rest of the flowers, then threaded his fingers in mine and pulled me close. "You, little boy, are loved."

▲

At eight, I squeezed myself into the Versace dress, threw on a faux-fur coat, and grabbed Alán's hand. We went out into the cold night toward Friend's Tavern. Jackson Heights was always busy, even on a Tuesday evening, and as we pounded through the crowded streets, we had to maneuver around families waiting in line at taco trucks, mariachis traveling from restaurant to restaurant taking song requests, passengers hurrying out of the crowded train station. Several of them turned their heads to gawk at me, clinging to Alán's arm for warmth.

Neither of us was sure what to expect from the launch. There was no budget, people in other parts of New York rarely came out to Queens, and yet stepping into Friend's, I knew right away everything had turned out exactly as it should have.

My eardrums nearly burst from the rowdy salsa music the DJ was playing as we headed to a back corner of the bar, where the team at Love Wins had set up a table with a tall stack of copies of my book, the glossy covers twinkling beneath the disco balls hanging from the ceiling. Next to the table was Daniel, one of the founders of the pantry. He greeted Alán and me by pouring us shots from a bottle of aguardiente that a shirtless Colombian bartender brought over in an ice bucket.

Not long after that, Paula, Love Wins' volunteer manager, pushed through the doors fresh from a shift at a local community garden. Soon Joseph arrived from Brooklyn, wearing a head-to-toe silk look and a dangly palm tree earring, followed by former co-workers from Industry, the reservations office in SoHo, and the Mexican restaurant I'd cashiered at when I first moved to the city. More and more of the friends I'd made over the past couple of years trickled in little by little, holding flower bouquets, thrusting pens into my hands so I could sign their copies of my book. The latest crop of Mirror students showed up fashionably late, trailing behind Lesly, whose forty-inch jet-black wig swished back and forth over her ass, hypnotizing the men seated along the bar. "¡Que perrrrra!" she screamed, feeling the fabric of my dress. "Is this real?"

"Duh!" I said. "I know a guy . . ."

Around midnight the DJ put on a J.Lo song, and we all rushed out onto the dance floor laughing. I twirled around in my dress, buzzed on too many aguardiente shots, the strobe lights painting our faces green and purple and blue. For a second, my publication worries vanished, and I let myself fully savor the moment: how long it'd taken to get here, how sweet it felt to know that all the days I'd been lost, I was headed the right way. And like it always happened when in a room full of dancing queer people, my chest ached for the Pulse victims who should have been alive to follow their dreams too. I closed my eyes and sent out a message of gratitude to wherever they were.

From behind, a pair of arms wrapped around my waist. I turned to find Alán beaming at me, his skin glowing with sweat. "You happy, baby?" he whispered in my ear.

It was a question he'd been asking me a lot lately, most recently while eating tamales on the couch. Usually I shrugged, made a dumb joke. Now I looked around the room, at everyone who'd come to celebrate, and I didn't feel like being funny.

"Yeah, I think so," I let myself say.

He rolled his eyes. "You *think* you are?"

I rested my forehead against his and focused on his goofy

smile, his soft, pink lips, until the sounds of the bar faded away and all that was left was him holding me. In an hour the party would be over and we'd have to go home again. It'd be just me and him, alone in our fake room.

"I am." I pressed my lips to his. "I definitely am. I'm happy."

Six months later, Alán and I were living in San Juan, Puerto Rico.

We were there so I could be nearer to my father. We had started talking more and more after I'd visited, sending each other voice notes and messages on WhatsApp. Mine were guarded at first: a photo of the dirty snow in New York, exclamation points when he responded with one of wild horses galloping on the beach in Vieques. Those were followed by calls after Hector's baby was born, the two of us marveling over how much she took after our side of the family. Papi kept asking when I would come back, and finally I caved. The pandemic had reminded me how precious life was. I'd wanted to make up for the time we'd lost, give us a real chance to have a relationship so the next generation could have one with him too.

Alán and I moved into a one-bedroom apartment on the second floor of a crumbling old building, in a neighborhood where the power went out daily and pigs roamed freely through the streets. Tourists pressed hard on their accelerators when they drove by in their rental cars, but I wouldn't have traded it for anything. We were minutes from the beach, on a block where everybody looked out for each other. Our neighbors dropped by all the time to trade plantains from our tree for gossip, or for a bite of whatever Mexican dish Alán was cooking. The woman who lived downstairs from us, Doña Celinda, was a big reader and frequently came up with dusty copies of poetry and rum for us to share. We'd sit on my balcony for hours, talking about all the artists she used to know when she was younger and worked as a book publicist. It was Doña Celinda who finally convinced me to suck it up and tell my mother what I'd written.

One week toward the end of summer, I flew to Orlando. The first couple of days I stalled, relishing in the ease of mornings in her garden, going on long drives together and taking in how much the city had changed since I'd left: the new chain restaurants, the housing developments that had sprouted up where there were once orange groves. Eventually I took her to a bookstore, bracing myself as I walked her up to the memoir aisle. When I found my book, I pulled it from the shelf, opened it to the dedication page, and showed her where it said, *For my mother, La Terrible* (her teenage nickname). I showed her how I'd made *Mom* the first word.

She seemed confused at first, then her eyes glossed over, a slow smile spread across her face, and she said, "Wow. I'm so proud of you, baby. I'm so proud!"

That night she took the copy I'd bought her into her room and closed the door behind her, while I lay on my childhood mattress in the room next to hers biting my nails. Her reaction when she finished was a little anticlimactic, considering how much time I'd spent agonizing over this moment. She said she thought the words I used were very pretty. She said the story moved her. She slapped my arm and said she wished I didn't tell people that she stole coffee for our family from Starbucks. "What if I try to get a job there again?!" I could tell there was something else she wanted to say, but she left it at that. Then she hugged me, hard.

Her approval meant more to me than any of the other successes the book had so far: the flattering reviews, the exciting national coverage. Publishing a book hadn't made me wealthy, but every morning I woke up feeling rich. I had my own place. A beautiful and kind man who loved me. I was the most stable I'd ever been, slowly building a career through teaching and writing, two things that made me feel useful and valued. Girl, I swore I was in the last ten minutes of a J.Lo rom-com.

On the flight back to San Juan from Orlando, the plane was full of Puerto Ricans: some who were born on the island, others who grew up in the diaspora. It's an old Puerto Rican tradition to break into applause once the plane arrives in PR, a tradition that acknowledges the pain of colonialism and what a thrill it is to return to the land. I've heard tourists complain about this, call it cringey. The older I get, the easier it is for me to tune those voices out. That day, as the plane touched down on the island and almost everyone around me clapped and called their families to tell them they'd made it, I just heard a lot of people who were glad to be home.

It was one of those hectic weekday afternoons when there was no time to breathe. It wasn't even one o'clock yet, and already I'd driven Doña Celinda on an errand, finished a draft of an article, washed a week's laundry by hand, answered a thousand emails, and booked my next ferry trip to see Papi in Vieques. I'd been sitting at my desk prepping for a class when my phone rang.

It was Mom. I was about to ask if I could call her later so I could finish what I was working on, but there was a strange heaviness to her voice that kept me on the line.

"Are you all right?" I asked.

She was quiet for a second, and then she said, "I'm sorry." Her apology caught me completely off guard. I thought I heard her sniffle and blow her nose. It sounded like she'd been crying. I got up and took the phone outside onto the balcony so that I could hear her better.

"Sorry for what?" I leaned against the railing. On the street below, a flock of chickens pecked at a bag of trash that had fallen out of a neighbor's dumpster.

"I've been thinking lately," Mom said, "about everything. I know I haven't always been a good mom, that there were times when we didn't have enough and I yelled at you or we fought. And I want to . . . to ask for your forgiveness."

I didn't know what to say, so I simply stood there and listened in shock. I couldn't believe we were having this conversation, now of all times, on a random weekday while I was in cutoff shorts and flip-flops. I'd tried to speak with her about the trauma of our pasts before, but those conversations never went well. Every time, she either stormed off or launched into one of her Latin Mom monologues about how much she'd sacrificed for us, that of course I wanted to make her out to be the bad guy. It wasn't that at all, rather that ignoring our trauma as if it didn't happen often made me feel delusional, like I'd made it up. How could either of us heal if we couldn't at least talk about what hurt? It's part of the reason I wrote my book, so that I could get out what I needed to say without her interrupting to tell me how ungrateful I was.

That's when it hit me: the book. She hadn't had to hear me out. She read all the things I hadn't been able to talk to her about, sat with them, and now she was apologizing. Suddenly I understood that this was what she'd wanted to tell me the day she'd finished it: *I'm sorry*.

"It's okay," I said. "You don't have to be sorry. I love you. That was a long time ago."

"Yes, it was." Mom's voice cracked over the phone. "But I have to tell you this."

I stared out to the end of the block, picturing her back in Orlando, lying in bed in one of her old floral-print nightgowns, a pile of soiled, crumpled-up tissues beside her.

"¿Cómo te lo explico?" she started. "When I came to this country, I had all these men saying they wanted to marry me, that they wanted to buy me this and that, but when I met your father . . ." She took a moment to collect herself, blowing her nose again. "I'd had boyfriends, nothing serious, but when I met your father, that was the first time I said yes, okay.

"It wasn't until after you were born that he changed. We were arguing all the time. Ay, como peleamos. . . . Your abuela wanted to kill him. I don't know where he was getting the drugs, but I begged him to stop. I gave him chance after chance, and then I had to get you away. I had to make sure you and Hector were safe. But after the divorce I was so depressed. It was just me and you kids, and you were so young and I—I was scared. I wasn't all the way there, you understand? All I could do was cry. They put me on so many pills that made me sick. You remember that? The doctors told me to rest, but I had to get back to work. I saw your little faces and it broke my heart, because who else was there? Who else would take care of you?"

"I know, Mamá," I reassured her. "I know. It wasn't fair you had to do it alone."

"I didn't mean to yell at you like I did. I didn't mean to make you sad. It wasn't right." She was sobbing now. "I kept trying to make things better but I just made everything worse. I could barely get through the day. The alarm would go off at three in the morning and I would force myself to wake up and go to work, but it was like someone else took over my body.

"And then you came home from school and told me they were kicking you out. And I tried to act fine, I went to the school and said please, he made a mistake, but inside I just thought of your father . . . how I couldn't let you become . . . I was scared you were going to get hurt, of the people you started hanging around with. You think I didn't know? I knew. I always knew, and everyone said to watch out, that you were not like the other boys, but please believe me, I'm sorry, I'm so sorry, all I ever wanted was for you to be happy."

"Mamá, I am," I said. "I'm happy because of you, because of what you did for us. You don't have to feel bad. I know you were doing your best. Even when we didn't have much, you always found ways to make every day special. Remember when we used to tour those timeshares so we could get tickets to Disney? And when you took me to get my teeth fixed and the dentist looked at us crazy when you pulled out all your cards?"

I heard her giggle softly to herself.

"There were bad memories, yes," I said. "But there were way more good ones. I love you, Mamá. I love you so much."

"I love you too," she said.

We spent another hour talking about all the things she regretted, how she wished our lives could have been different. I promised her I didn't blame her for the past, that if I'd had a choice, I would have picked her to be my mom again and again. By the time we'd both gotten everything off our chests, the flock of chickens downstairs had moved on up the road, leaving in their wake a trail of torn plastic bags and takeout containers. They were monsters. Making messes everywhere. But I always felt lucky in the mornings when I woke up to them singing.

"I have an idea," I told her. "What if from this day forward, we start over? All that happened back then is in the past. From here on out, a fresh start."

"A new chapter?" she asked.

I shook my head, laughing. "Yeah, a new chapter."

"Okay," she said. "Deal."

The following afternoon, though, I couldn't get the suspicion that there was more to her sudden outburst of emotions out of my head. It was obvious to me that something had triggered her, something other than just my book, so I called her to make sure she was still all right.

"¡Ay!" She brushed my question away. "I'm fine! Don't worry about me! I can't call and speak to my son?"

But I wouldn't let it go.

Twenty minutes later I finally got out of her that the bank had sent her a letter threatening to take possession of her house because she'd fallen "slightly behind" on payments.

"Those people," she scoffed. "They're always sending me letters. I'll figure it out. They can't just take the house. They have to warn you."

"Mamá," I said as gently as I could, "I think those letters are the warnings."

"Are you sure?" she asked, sounding more concerned.

Like me, my mother wasn't one to ask for help. It was important for her to be self-sufficient. When she had cancer a few years earlier, she didn't tell my brother and me until after she'd had the tumor removed. I knew she'd been struggling since being let go from Starbucks, but I'd assumed the disability checks she was receiving were enough to pay her rent.

I pressed her to tell me more, and she nervously explained that they had been enough for a while, but then her insurance rates went up, and now they weren't. And because my mother is my mother, in the pandemic she'd been putting everything on cards so she could send money to her brother's widow and children in Nicaragua. It had all caught up to her. She had over $30,000 in overdue credit card debt. Interest charges were racking up. The bank was gunning for her house. And even if she tried to get another job, she was a chronically ill woman in her late fifties whose only work experience in decades was being a barista. "It's going to be okay, you'll see," she said, but beneath the calm exterior she was putting on, she was clearly rattled.

I didn't care about the money or the house. All I could think was that her Bell's palsy had already returned once. What would this additional stress do to her while she was still rebuilding her health? My mind flashed back to when I was twelve, standing at the foot of her bed, afraid to call an ambulance because of what it would cost. I couldn't freeze up again.

When the call ended, despite her repeatedly insisting I shouldn't worry, I promised I'd find a way to help. I left the apartment an anxious wreck, not sure how I was going to deliver on my promise. I'd been sending her what I could—my food stamps when I got those, a couple hundred dollars here and there—but I'd only just stopped struggling to pay my own bills. I had no savings. No jewelry stashed away or anything of monetary value I could sell. Between writing and teaching, I made around $2,000 a month. I was barely getting by myself.

In the street outside my apartment building, I began to walk aimlessly, trying to think about how I could stretch my next paycheck, my surroundings closing in on me as the shock set in. All this time I'd believed the worst days were behind us, and oh my god, we weren't even close. If anything, we were almost back to where we'd started. How could I be so stupid? Living the last few months as if I were in some fantasy happy ending, like I was the only one this was about, like it was really going to be that easy.

Before I knew where my legs were taking me, I was at the beach, tripping through the heavy sand, past people sunbathing and kids playing on the shore, waves crashing beyond them. I waded into the water, desperate to be somewhere quieter, then dove in headfirst and swam, kicking and kicking until I was out in the ocean, my arms growing weaker with each stroke, the muscles in my legs burning. But the cool water felt good against my skin. So I kept swimming.

She's right, I told myself. *It's going to be okay. I just have to make more money.* I pushed and kicked harder. *Find more work. A third or fourth job.* Forget writing. Teaching. Who cared about my dreams? What about my mom's? What about the dreams she'd sacrificed for me? In the meantime, I could put all my expenses on my cards, send her money sooner. Tackle the interest charges first. That was the most urgent. Fuck. No, her house. I could ask my landlord for an extension on this month's rent. In fact, I could give up the apartment and my life in Puerto Rico completely. Would Alán come, if I moved to Florida to stay with her and save for a few months? A year? If he didn't, then . . . I don't know . . . then maybe that was . . . then maybe some people get to be happy and some people don't and that's just how it is.

My arms were tensing up. My lungs were starved for air. I lifted my head from the water, gasping.

There was nothing but blue on all sides, no sign of anyone nearby. It was the farthest out I'd ever been. Panic swept through me as I tried to stay afloat, my legs kicking furiously beneath me. I turned to where I thought the shore was. I had to get back. But I was so tired. The ocean below so dark, quiet down there, peaceful. I felt my strength leaving me. My body sinking.

Then I remembered something from a long time ago, something I learned as a kid swimming in the beaches of Florida. If you ever feel like you're about to drown, you're supposed to lie on your back and let the water carry you until you're ready to keep going again. It wasn't much, but it was everything.

I stopped kicking, spread my arms, and floated on my back. I finally accepted that I couldn't do it on my own.

A few days later, after talking through our options with my mother, we'd create an emergency GoFundMe page for her. Within a week, she'd receive over $30,000 in donations, the majority of them in small five- and ten-dollar increments from queer readers who wanted to extend a little kindness to the woman they'd met in my book. At our weakest, hundreds of people would show up to rescue us from drowning. They'd remind us that strength doesn't mean suffering in silence. It means being in community.

"I don't understand," Mom would say, crying on the phone as I gave her the news that we had enough to save her house, to pay off some bills, that we didn't have to be afraid anymore. "Is this real? I've been praying, but I didn't . . . I never imagined . . . How do I say thank you?"

"It's real, Mamá," I'd tell her through my own tears. "People love you. I'll let them know you're happy."

The sun warmed my face as I floated on the water, letting the waves carry me for a while. There was still a long way to go, so I closed my eyes and rested.

Right then, that's what I needed to do to survive.

ACKNOWLEDGMENTS

Mamá, La Terrible, la quiero mucho. Thank you for modeling for me how to be resourceful, courageous, and for trusting me with this story. Hector, thank you for all the good things you do and don't tell anyone about, for walking the walk. Arturo, thank you for being there for me always, even when we're thousands of miles away from each other. Luis, thank you for being the blueprint. Joseph, thank you for knocking on my bedroom door in the pandemic. Elyse, thank you for being down to make silly videos with me and for being the funniest person I know. Jason, thank you for all the family meals and the afternoons on your couch. Kyla, thank you for talking to me on the bus my first day at Oak Ridge. Eryn, thank you for your gentle, but needed, makeup advice. Erika, thank you for opening up your life to me in Jackson Heights. Viva Casa Gabriel! José Fernando, Paca, thank you for being my family in Puerto Rico. Paula, thank you for welcoming me to Love Wins and for our cafecito walks through the neighborhood.

To the volunteers and organizers at Love Wins Food Pantry and the Mirror Beauty Co-operative: Daniel. Mark. Brian. Day. Claudia. Ruth. Carly. Joana. Lesly. Joselyn. So many others. Thank you for teaching me how to fight for the world I want to live in.

To my writing group: Asha French. Minda Honey. Natalie Lima. Elizabeth Owuor. Natassja Schiel. Thank you for lending your thoughtful eyes to my words. I feel so lucky to know you.

Danielle. The best agent in the world. Thank you for changing my life. Again.

Aubrey. Thank you for seeing the potential in a book about Florida, for your brilliant guidance, and for offering me a happy ending that goes beyond this story.

Thank you to the team at Crown who helped make this into a real book. Liana Faughnan. Amani Shakrah. Anna Kochman. Dustin Amick. Janet Biehl. Andrea C. Peabbles. Eldes Tran. Sibylle Kazeroid. Miriam Taveras. Julie Cepler. Rachel Rodriguez. Dyana Messina. Bree Martinez. Thank you to Arsh Raziuddin for the cover design.

Thank you to the Black Mountain Institute for supporting

my writing (Hey, Kim!) with a Shearing fellowship, a place to stay, and that gooood unlimited printer access.

I don't even know how to begin thanking everyone who donated to or shared my mom's GoFundMe. Rigoberto González. Roxane Gay. Vanessa Chan. Laila Lalami. Your generosity inspires me. I promise to pay it forward. All the people who donated whatever you could, you saved my family more than you will ever know. Red Lobster is on me the second I'm rich.

And Alán. Thank you for reminding me to eat, for being a daily source of comfort, for showing me money isn't everything. Thank you for making a home with me, wherever we are. I love you. And I'm still mad you were late.

About the Author

EDGAR GOMEZ (He/They) is the author of *High-Risk Homosexual,* which received an American Book Award, a Stonewall–Israel Fishman Honor Award, and the Lambda Literary Award for Gay Memoir. Born and raised in Florida, he has written for the *Los Angeles Times, Poets & Writers, LitHub, New York* magazine, and beyond. His work has been supported by the National Endowment for the Arts, the New York Foundation for the Arts, and the Black Mountain Institute. Gomez lives in New York and Puerto Rico.